The Vermont Quiz Book

Compiled and Edited
by
Frank Bryan
Melissa Lee Bryan

The New England Press
Shelburne, Vermont

©1986 by Frank M. Bryan and Melissa Lee Bryan
ALL RIGHTS RESERVED

ISBN 0-933050-43-7
Library of Congress Catalog Card Number: 86-62544
Printed in the United States of America
Design by Andrea Gray
First Edition

For additional copies, please write:
The New England Press
P.O. Box 575
Shelburne, Vermont 05482

For Rachel and Frank
good kids

Acknowledgments

Special thanks go to the following: First and foremost, to the many public managers in Vermont's state government, especially those in the Departments of Agriculture, Education, Fish and Wildlife, and Motor Vehicles, the Agency of Development and Community Affairs, the Project Planning Division of the Agency of Transportation, and most importantly, to Greg Sanford and Marjorie Strong at the State Papers Division of the Secretary of State's Office. The staff of Special Collections at the University of Vermont's Bailey–Howe Library was always friendly and helpful. The Vermont Institute of Natural Science (for its *Newsletter*) and the Vermont Historical Society (for *Vermont History* and the *Green Mountaineer*) were most helpful. *Vermont Life* magazine was both a tremendous help and a curse, since we spent so much time indulging ourselves the thorough enjoyment of re-reading old issues! Besides the deep gratitude we owe the authors of the many books and articles that serve as source material for the book, we wish to thank Phil Ambrose, Clark Bensen, David Bryan, Jean Cate, Jeff Cedarfield, Peter and Melanie Cole, John and Irene Currie, Don Fillion, Marie Geno, Emory Hebard, Jim Pacy, John Smith, Kendall Wild, Jym Wilson, and of course Al Rosa and Paul Eschholz at the New England Press. To Jeff Olson, who shepherded the volume through production and who edited each and every question and answer, a special thank you.

Contents

Introduction

This began (we admit it) as another trivia book. But it quickly became something else. Is there *anything* trivial about Vermont? We suppose so. For instance, what is Madeleine Kunin's middle name? But there is so much more about Vermont that's interesting, important, fun, and that still provides the little burst of ego that comes with the recognition: *I knew that!*

Even if you're not sure of the answer, the Vermonter in you should challenge you to take a stab at it, and if you still miss it, we hope the question itself is enticing enough to make the answer irresistible. Accordingly, we often spent as much time explaining the answer as we did in asking the question. For instance, why was Thaddeus Stevens expelled from the University of Vermont? You may not know, but we guarantee the answer will surprise you.*

In reviewing other quiz and trivia books, we were struck by the nakedness of the format and the information provided. Norman Cousins, longtime editor and essayist for the *Saturday Review*, commenting on the human factor in learning, said in his 1981 volume *Human Options*: "If we want knowledge without values, we can find it in almanacs. If we want information without motivation, we can get it in computers." We have therefore tried to add a human touch to this book—values and motivation. Thus while answering a question on spring wildflowers, we included part of a poem we like. In answering a question on leg-hold traps, we offered an opinion. Often we tried to share the passion of a Robert Rogers, the courage of a Seth Hubbell, the wisdom of a George Aiken. Even the pictures reflect our values. We took

*You may not even remember who Thaddeus Stevens was. Not to worry—we'll fill you in.

them ourselves, and not as photographers but as Vermonters with a camera.

Furthermore, we wanted this book to be educational as well as fun. Don't panic. We are both teachers, and we both believe education *can* be fun. It is fun to know, and it is fun to be (mildly) competitive about learning. Someone once said that the true mark of educated people is that they know how much they don't know. After constructing over sixteen hundred questions about Vermont, we have come to realize how much there is to know, *really* know, about the Green Mountain State. If we've been at all successful with this book, then you should have the same reaction we did—"Whew . . . I didn't realize there was so much to know!"

John Dewey, himself a Vermonter, once observed that the total educational experience for an entire year of a child's schooling ought to be focused on one thing, a grand focal point from which all learning—math, history, art, whatever—would be drawn. Not a bad idea. Could there be a better theme than Vermont? For example, we have included a question about the number of miles one would have to travel to walk completely around Lake Champlain. What's involved? Geography, arithmetic, a little history, geometry—you name it. Vermont is a prism through which the colors of learning dance and sparkle and delight like dew on the dandelions of a morning mountainside in May.

One more thing. We believe knowledge is love. The phrase "familiarity breeds contempt" was penned by a pessimist condemned forever to wake in the morning committed to either stupidity or depression. To know Vermont is to love it. This book, then, is for lovers, Vermont-lovers.

CHAPTER 1

Who Are Those Guys, Anyway?

Many have tried to map that rugged territory called the Vermont "character." Its precise dimensions remain, however, a mystery. Yet, like the topography of this most rural state, the general contours are everywhere evident. They are contained in the notions of liberty spawned in and by community, the courage and wisdom to take democracy seriously, personal independence and self-reliance, a faith in the work ethic, and fidelity to the truth that every individual is a free person with the right to be a saint or a damned fool and that this capacity for free will radiates a special dignity reserved only for the human race.

The fifty persons listed below—some living, some dead, some born in Vermont, others not—all share in some respect (like the others found in this volume) a common denominator spelled V-E-R-M-O-N-T-E-R. We have clustered them in five groups of ten and simply ask you to match their names with the characteristics with which they are associated.

The answers to Chapter 1 begin on page 4.

1

Group A

_____	1. Allen R. Foley	a. Auctioneer
_____	2. Elizabeth Candon	b. Sculptor
_____	3. Dwight J. Dwinell	c. Bureaucrat, Conservationist
_____	4. Arthur Packard	d. Humorist, Professor
_____	5. Perry Merrill	e. Sergeant-at-Arms
_____	6. Harland Tatro	f. Printmaker
_____	7. Deborah Clifford	g. Newspaper Editor
_____	8. M. Dickey Drysdale	h. Educator, Bureaucrat
_____	9. Hiram Powers	i. Historian: Vermont Women
_____	10. Mary Azarian	j. Vermont Farm Bureau

Group B

_____	11. Weston Cate	a. Scholar of Public Administration
_____	12. Marshall Dimock	b. Old-time Fiddler
_____	13. Olin Maxham	c. Librarian
_____	14. Vivian Bryan*	d. Auditor of Accounts
_____	15. Jeff Danziger	e. Vermont Country Store
_____	16. Vrest Orton	f. Women's Education
_____	17. Alexander Acebo	g. Ox Teamster
_____	18. Blanche Honegger Moyse	h. Former Vermont Historical Society Director
_____	19. Emma Willard	i. Promoter of Classical Music, Windham County
_____	20. Wilfred Guillette	j. Cartoonist

Group C

_____	21. Philip Brooks	a. College President
_____	22. Louise McCarren	b. Poet
_____	23. Dorothy Canfield Fisher	c. Novelist–Conservationist
_____	24. Daisy Dopp	d. Columnist in the Kingdom
_____	25. Harold Blaisdell	e. Legislator–Bureaucrat
_____	26. Richard Mallary	f. Town Manager
_____	27. Caroline A. Yale	g. Educating the Deaf
_____	28. "Corky" Elwell	h. Outdoorsman and Writer
_____	29. Royce S. Pitkin	i. Taxidermist
_____	30. John Engels	j. Public Service Board

*no relation

Group D

_____ 31. Janice Ryan   a. Vermont Humorist

_____ 32. Francis Colburn   b. Eco-Libertarian

_____ 33. Walter Hard   c. State Legislator, Burlington

_____ 34. Murray Bookchin   d. Vermont Historian:

_____ 35. John Dewey   Place–Names

_____ 36. Herbert Ogden   e. Literary Critic, Orleans

_____ 37. Jim Hayford   f. Educationalist–Philosopher

_____ 38. Esther Swift   g. State Legislator, Hartland

_____ 39. Esther J. Urie   h. Schoolteacher

_____ 40. Lorraine Graham   i. College President

                                        j. Poet of the Vermont Character

Group E

_____ 41. Ann Story   a. The Brattleboro Retreat

_____ 42. Susan Howard Webb   b. Artist

_____ 43. Chester Nutting   c. Novelist

_____ 44. Elmer Towne   d. State Legislator, Plymouth

_____ 45. Reid Lefevre   e. Pioneer and Green

_____ 46. Ely Culbertson   Mountain "Boy"

_____ 47. Mrs. Lisle McIntosh   f. "Bridge for Peace"

_____ 48. Luigi Lucioni   g. Showman and Legislator

_____ 49. Howard Mosher   h. Bureaucrat, Agriculturalist

_____ 50. Anna Hunt Marsh   i. Woodcarver

                                        j. Mincemeat Maker

Answers:
Who Are Those Guys, Anyway?

Group A

1. d. Allen R. Foley — Humorist, professor at Dartmouth, author of *What the Old-Timer Said.*
2. h. Elizabeth Candon — Educator, Bureaucrat, Sister of Mercy.
3. e. Dwight J. Dwinell — Sergeant-at-Arms, State House, for twenty-two years. At the age of eighty-seven, he directed the creation of Ceres II and its placement on the State House in 1938.
4. j. Arthur Packard — Vermont Farm Bureau, lobbyist, organizer of Neighborhood Club Forums.
5. c. Perry Merrill — Bureaucrat, conservationist, author.
6. a. Harland Tatro — Auctioneer, Alburg.
7. i. Deborah Clifford — Historian, scholar of political activism among Vermont women.
8. g. M. Dickey Drysdale — Newspaper editor, the *White River Valley Herald* in Randolph.
9. b. Hiram Powers — Sculptor. His most famous creation: the "Greek Slave."
10. f. Mary Azarian — Printmaker, Plainfield. She created *A Farmer's Alphabet* and *The Tale of John Barleycorn.*

Group B

11. h. Weston Cate — Director, Vermont Historical Society, January 1975–August 1985.
12. a. Marshall Dimock — Leading national scholar and author in the field of public administration, Bethel resident.
13. g. Olin Maxham — Ox teamster and man of the country, from South Woodstock.
14. c. Vivian Bryan — Librarian, Vermont State Library, Montpelier.
15. j. Jeff Danziger — Cartoonist and Vermont humorist, Plainfield.
16. e. Vrest Orton — Owner, Vermont Country Store.
17. d. Alexander Acebo — Auditor of Accounts, state of Vermont.
18. i. Blanche Honegger Moyse — Promoter of classical music, Windham County. She also helped found the fa-

4

mous Marlboro Festival of Music along with Rudolf Serkin, and Louis and Marcel Moyse.

19. f.	Emma Willard	— Pioneer in women's education in America, Middlebury resident.
20. b.	Wilfred Guillette	— Old-time fiddler, carpenter, Derby.

Group C

21. i.	Philip Brooks	— Taxidermist, Glover.
22. j.	Louise McCarren	— Chairman, Public Service Board.
23. c.	Dorothy Canfield Fisher	— Writer, novelist, conservationist
24. d.	Daisy Dopp	— Northeast Kingdom newspaper columnist. Elka Schumann calls her "one of the memorable citizens of Vermont's Northeast Kingdom."
25. h.	Harold Blaisdell	— He was one of Vermont's best-known outdoorsmen. He wrote four books on fishing in Vermont including *The Philosophical Fisherman* and *Tricks That Take Fish*.
26. e.	Richard Mallary	— Politician, farmer, public administrator, from Fairlee.
27. g.	Caroline A. Yale	— World leader in education for the deaf. Born in Charlotte, she served for fifty years as head of the Clarke School for the Deaf in Northampton, Massachusetts. Caroline Sweet of Woodstock and Gertrude Croker of Brattleboro were also Vermonters known for their work in education for the deaf.
28. f.	"Corky" Elwell	— Town manager, Brattleboro, for twenty-six years.
29. a.	Royce S. Pitkin	— Founder and president of Goddard College.
30. b.	John Engels	— Vermont poet, professor of English at St. Michael's College. His books of verse include *The Seasons in Vermont* and *The Homer Mitchell Place*.

Group D

31. i.	Janice Ryan	— Trinity College president.
32. a.	Francis Colburn	— Humorist, famous for the "Graduation Address" and several record albums of Vermont humor.

33. j. Walter Hard — Vermont poet, known for his descriptions of Vermont people and as owner of the Johnny Appleseed Bookshop in Manchester. When he died at age eighty-four he had written nine volumes of poetry and two of prose.

34. b. Murray Bookchin — Eco-libertarian, author and scholar.

35. f. John Dewey — Leading American educational philosopher, author of *Democracy in Education* and many other books.

36. g. Herbert Ogden — Vermont state senator, 1973–1980, from Hartland.

37. e. Jim Hayford — Poet, schoolteacher, literary critic from Orleans.

38. d. Esther Swift — Vermont historian from Royalton. A sixth-generation Vermonter who wrote, among other volumes, *Vermont Place-Names*, a prodigious effort in the Vermont tradition of painstaking care and excellence.

39. h. Esther J. Urie — Prominent Vermont schoolteacher for forty years.

40. c. Lorraine Graham — State legislator, Burlington.

Group E

41. e. Ann Story — Pioneer famous for her remark to the Green Mountain Boys: "Give me a place among you, and see if I am the first to desert my post."

42. d. Susan Howard Webb — State legislator, Plymouth.

43. i. Chester Nutting — Woodcarver. Other famous Vermont carvers are Edmond Menard (taught by Nutting), Herbert Wilcox, and Frank Moran of Bakersfield, known as the "woodcarver of Little Egypt."

44. h. Elmer Towne — Long-time Vermont Commissioner of Agriculture. Born in Waterbury Center in 1899 on a small dairy farm, he became a major force in Vermont agriculture in the 1940's and 1950's.

45. g. Reid Lefevre — Member of Vermont Legislature from Manchester. One of the most colorful politicians in Vermont in the 1950's. He was a world-traveled showman who was

6

memorialized by Norman Rockwell in
the *Saturday Evening Post.*

46. f. Ely Culbertson — "Bridge for Peace." He lived in Barnard,
Vermont. His books on bridge (the card
game) were the best-selling non-fiction
books in America next to the Bible in
the 1930's and 1940's. As a major force
in the peace movement of his day and
head of the Citizens Committee for
United Nations Reform, he fought for
world disarmament and control of
atomic weapons.

47. j. Mrs. Lisle McIntosh — Mincemeat maker of South Royalton.
She became a legend throughout New
England. In 1950 at the age of eighty-six
she "put up" 4½ tons of mincemeat, got
into a truck and sold it on the road for
cash.

48. b. Luigi Lucioni — Artist, has been called "painter laureate" of Vermont.

49. c. Howard Mosher — Novelist. If you wonder why Ken Kesey
(*One Flew Over the Cuckoo's Nest* and
Sometimes a Great Notion) has said of
Mosher's *Disappearances* " . . . one hell
of a book! A wonderful book, a terrible
book. It touches the vein of Hawthorne
and Poe, running deep in the American
fear and the American hope," then read
how Howard Mosher finishes a story.
From his novel about life in the Northeast Kingdom, *Disappearances*: "The
sun was rising, glinting off Rene's
musket, shining on the snow, illuminat-
ing the swamp, Kingdom County, Vermont and Quebec. Downriver a loon
hooted, its long wild call floated over
the water and trees and snow as I stood
with empty arms on the edge of my
youth in a place wheeling sunward, full
of terror, full of wonder."

50. a. Anna Hunt Marsh — Was a leader in attempts to free mental
patients from harsh and cruel treatment.
Born in 1769 in Vernon, she left $10,000
in her will to begin what is now the
Brattleboro Retreat.

51.

Provide the caption for the above press photo.

a. The Wicked Witch of the West visits Vermont.
b. Poverty in Vermont: Montpelier bag lady caught stealing maple sap.
c. Leader of new Vermont religion, the Holy Sapsuckers, blesses the church's sacraments.
d. Sen. Mary Just Skinner arrested for impersonating Governor Kunin impersonating a Real Vermonter.
e. Governor Kunin being Governor Kunin.

Answer

e. Governor Kunin being Governor Kunin.

CHAPTER 2

The 251 Club
Vermont Towns

In Vermont towns lies the spirit of public life. Even though some of our towns have become cities, we are still apt to think of them the old way, as towns. There is even a club in Vermont made up of persons who have visited all of Vermont's cities and towns (and even some places that used to be towns). Our towns reflect our history. They are a compass to travel by. They sponsor our cherished political structure, town meeting. Often their names are unique and colorful.

Speaking of color, there is only one town whose name is (in total) a color of the spectrum. Can you name it?   52. _____

There are four other towns, however, whose names start with a color. What are they?

53. _____   55. _____

54. _____   56. _____

Some Vermont towns have the names of foreign countries like, for instance, Jamaica. Two others are (57.) _____ and (58.) _____. One town, (59.) _____ has the name of a capital of a foreign country* and nine (60.) _____, (61.) _____, (62.) _____, (63.) _____, (64.) _____, (65.) _____, (66.) _____,

*Nope, it is not Moscow. Moscow, Vermont, is not a town. Nor is it a village. It is, like "Beecher Falls," just a place.

The answers to Chapter 2 begin on page 15.

(67.) _____, and (68.) _____ have the names of capitals of American states. Many towns are named the same as very big cities outside Vermont. What is the largest American city that has the same name as a Vermont town? (69.) _____.

(70.) _____ and (71.) _____ are the only two Vermont towns with the name of an American state.

Four Vermont towns have names with clear biblical ties. Name them.

72. _____   74. _____

73. _____   75. _____

Many Vermont town names remind you of other things. Below are listed several items that remind us of town names. Can you name the town?

76. Henry David Thoreau   _____

77. Cigarettes   _____

78. A fruit associated with Georgia*   _____

79. The "thrill of . . . "   _____

80. . . . and the Dragon   _____

Some towns remind one of England and our British heritage. Burke, Vermont, for instance, has the same name as an important English political philosopher. Can you name the Vermont towns that have the same name as

81. a British general in World War II?   _____

82. a major British university?   _____

83. a famous English seventeenth-century poet?   _____

The name of some Vermont towns can be associated with position, such as *Top*sham. Name four others that have *under*, *over*, *high*, or *low* as a separate syllable (that is, *Sunder*land, *Glover*, *Dover*, *Bellows* Falls, and *Lowell* would not count):

Under and Over	*High and Low*
84. _____	86. _____
85. _____	87. _____

Directions on the compass are traditionally associated with place names,

*Those of you who said Jimmy Carter should be ashamed.

such as East Haven and Northfield. In Vermont, however, "West" is most commonly used. Complete the following lists:

<table>
<tr><td>Single-Word Towns
Incorporating "West"
such as <u>Weston</u></td><td>Double-Word Towns
Incorporating "West"
such as <u>West Windsor</u></td></tr>
</table>

88. _____   92. _____

89. _____   93. _____

90. _____   94. _____

91. _____

Town names often incorporate the names of natural and man-made objects. Maid*stone*, Tun*bridge*, Guild*hall*, and *Brook*line are examples. In Vermont, however, "field" is most popular.* There are thirteen of them.

Hint:	Town:
"a butcher, a . . ."	reminds us of <u>Bakersfield</u>

95. the . . . is off the rose   _____

96. . . . Shields   _____

97. "My . . . Lady"   _____

98. ". . . to Alaska"   _____

99. ". . . Jane"   _____

100. My compliments to the . . .   _____

101. Hurry up and . . .   _____

102. The . . . forecast   _____

103. "In . . . a young man's fancy turns to love."   _____

104. . . . mallows   _____

105. This place is the . . .   _____

106. "Go . . . young man."   _____

Many Vermont towns have men's first names. Name them using the hints provided.

---

*Perhaps because the early settlers spent their lives fashioning fields from the forests.

11

	Town:	*Hint:*

107. _____ An Allen

108. _____ A Peak

109. _____ A Chief Justice

110. _____ Gunsmoke

111. _____ A Chevy Chase character

112. _____ Benjamin

113. _____ A "Gap"

114. _____ Friedman (the economist)

115. _____ Patty Hearst's father

116. _____ Donahue (the actor)

117. _____ "ka-boom"

118. _____ 36th President of the U.S.

What about towns that used to be? One had the same name as a famous bull, (119.) _____. Another, the middle name of an author, W. (120.) _____ Maugham, and another the last name of a great heavyweight boxer, (121.) _____.

122. Several Vermont towns have the same names as former governors. Chittenden and Proctor are examples. Of the several that remain, name one: _____.

Above is a picture of Dorset Mountain. You are on Route 7 traveling in what direction?

123. _____

Below is a picture taken as you are traveling on Route 30 along the West River. The bridge spanning the road and the river carries what highway?

124. _____

Above is a picture of property owned by
(125). _____. What town is it in?
126. _____

The children splashing in this pool are in the center of
(127.) _____ city.

Answers:
The 251 Club

52. Orange
53. Brownington
54. Greensboro
55. Whiting
56. Whitingham. (We can't really count Reading, and White River Junction is not a town.)
57. Peru
58. Holland. OK, so Holland isn't technically a country, it's a province of the Netherlands. Most Vermonters know Holland as that nice country in Europe with the windmills and tulips. Close enough.
59. Athens, capital of Greece. (We didn't include Berlin because there is no Berlin; Germany now only has West Berlin and East Berlin, unfortunately. Also, many Vermonters may have said Washington. But, technically anyway, we have to concede that Washington, D.C., is not the capital of a foreign country.)
60. Montgomery, capital of Alabama.
61. Hartford, capital of Connecticut.
62. Dover, capital of Delaware.
63. Springfield, capital of Illinois.
64. Lincoln, capital of Nebraska.
65. Concord, capital of New Hampshire.
66. Albany, capital of New York.
67. Richmond, capital of Virginia.
68. Charleston, capital of West Virginia.
69. Baltimore
70. Georgia
71. Washington
72. Jericho
73. Eden
74. Canaan
75. Goshen
76. Walden
77. Marlboro
78. Peacham
79. Victory
80. St. George
81. Montgomery
82. Cambridge
83. Milton

84. *Under*hill
85. And*over*
86. *High*gate
87. Lud*low*
88. Westmore
89. Westfield
90. Westford
91. Westminster
92. West Fairlee
93. West Haven
94. West Rutland
95. Bloomfield
96. Brookfield
97. Fairfield
98. Northfield
99. Plainfield
100. Sheffield
101. Waitsfield
102. Weathersfield
103. Springfield
104. Marshfield
105. Pittsfield
106. Westfield

107. Ira
108. Jay
109. Warren
110. Chester
111. Fletcher
112. Franklin
113. Lincoln
114. Milton
115. Randolph
116. Troy
117. Vernon
118. Lyndon
119. Ferdinand
120. Somerset
121. Lewis
122. Either Fletcher, Johnson, or Woodbury
123. south
124. I–91
125. the state of Vermont
126. Waterbury
127. St. Albans

128.

In Vermont we name more after our mountains than anything else. The commercial establishment especially likes to use their name. Yet there is only one vegetable that has a variety named Green Mountain. It is?

a. A bean
b. Corn
c. A pea
d. A potato

Answer

d. The Green Mountain is a potato.

CHAPTER 3

Vermont and That Other State

"Anything I can say about New
Hampshire can be said as well
about Vermont. Excepting that they
differ in their mountains. The Vermont mountains stretch extended
straight; New Hampshire mountains (129.) _____

_____ _____ _____

_____."

Robert Frost

Vermonters have always claimed an ability to tell the difference between Vermont and New Hampshire. Indeed, the differences are many. But often it takes a well-honed Vermont consciousness to detect them. They are not all as blatant, for instance, as the presidential election of 1840 when Vermonters voted for Harrison two to one, while across the river our New England neighbors in New Hampshire voted three to one for Van Buren. Historian of the period Richard P. McCormick called it a "conundrum." The following questions test your knowledge of Vermont and New Hampshire as a pair of very different oxen that as Frost said share a geographical yoke —the back country of the Northeast.

Which State	Vermont	New Hampshire
130. has higher taxes?	_____	_____
131. has more lawyers per capita?	_____	_____
132. has more rainy days in June?	_____	_____
133. has the higher per capita gross state product?	_____	_____

The answers to Chapter 3 begin on page 21.

Which State	Vermont	New Hampshire
134. had the higher voter turnout in the 1984 Presidential election?	_____	_____
135. contains Mt. Lafayette?	_____	_____
136. is geographically larger?	_____	_____
137. has higher mountains?	_____	_____
138. is the birthplace of Sherman Adams?	_____	_____
139. has the larger population?	_____	_____
140. spends more per pupil for education?	_____	_____
141. has the larger percentage of land owned by the federal government?	_____	_____
142. voted for Roosevelt in 1936?	_____	_____
143. has the higher divorce rate?	_____	_____
144. has the higher number of murders per 100,000 people?	_____	_____
145. has the higher auto theft rate?	_____	_____
146. had the higher population increase from 1970–1980?	_____	_____
147. appropriates more state funds per capita for the arts?	_____	_____
148. has the higher percentage of population having completed 4 or more years of college?	_____	_____
149. is prettier?	_____	_____
150. has the larger state legislature?	_____	_____
151. spends more in state and local expenditures as a percentage of total personal income?	_____	_____
152. has an Ivy League college?	_____	_____
153. is the home of Yankee magazine?	_____	_____

154. has the higher per capita income?   _____   _____

155. has Bretton Woods?   _____   _____

156. has more miles of I–89?   _____   _____

157. has colder Februaries?   _____   _____

158. has the higher high-school graduation rate?   _____   _____

159. is longer?   _____   _____

160. has more adults under correctional supervision per 10,000 people?   _____   _____

161. contains Grafton County?   _____   _____

162. has more dairy farms?   _____   _____

163. has the largest lake completely within its borders?   _____   _____

164. had the higher cost of living in 1980?   _____   _____

165. consumed more energy per capita in 1983?   _____   _____

166. was the birthplace of Daniel Webster?   _____   _____

167. was the site of the Oscar-winning *On Golden Pond*?   _____   _____

168. has the higher suicide rate?   _____   _____

169. has more food-stamp recipients per 1,000 population?   _____   _____

170. pays their state legislators more?   _____   _____

171. had more chickens in 1982?   _____   _____

172. has the higher infant mortality rate?   _____   _____

173. is more dependent on federal aid?   _____   _____

174. Are the mountains in the background of the picture above White
Mountains or Green Mountains?

Answers:
Vermont and That Other State

129. curl up in a coil
130. Vermont. In 1984 Vermont ranked near the top (among the 50 states) on state and local taxes per $1,000 of personal income. New Hampshire ranked at the absolute bottom (#50). Vermonters paid $121.77 of every $1,000 earned. New Hampshire's citizens paid only $89.35 of every $1,000 earned.
131. Vermont. In 1980 there was one lawyer for every 467 men, women, and children in Vermont. In New Hampshire there was one for every 549.
132. Vermont. On average New Hampshire has 11. Vermont has 12. Actually the U.S. Statistical Abstract only reports readings from the Concord and Burlington weather stations—the state-wide totals may vary.
133. New Hampshire. In 1982 the total market value of all final goods and services produced in Vermont was $5,237,000,000 ($10,289 per capita). New Hampshire's was $10,851,000,000 ($11,782 per capita).
134. Vermont, 60.1% to 53.9% of voting-age population casting votes.
135. New Hampshire.
136. Vermont, 9,609 square miles to 9,304.
137. New Hampshire. Mt. Washington at 6,288 feet is more than a thousand feet higher than Vermont's Mt. Mansfield.
138. Vermont. Sherman Adams, the often controversial advisor to President Eisenhower between 1952 and 1958, was often called by the press the "assistant president."
139. New Hampshire. In 1980 it was 920,600 to 511,456.
140. Vermont. In 1982 Vermont spent $2,365 and New Hampshire spent $2,256.
141. The "Feds" own 12.8% of New Hampshire and 5.4% of Vermont.
142. New Hampshire.
143. New Hampshire.
144. Vermont. In 1983 and 1984 Vermont "led" by about two to one.
145. New Hampshire. In 1984, 189 thefts were reported per 100,000 population. In Vermont it was 155.
146. New Hampshire, 24.8% to 15.0%.
147. Vermont gave 42 cents per person in 1984. New Hampshire coughed up 13 cents.
148. Vermont, 19% to 18%.
149. Whoaback!

150. New Hampshire has the largest of any state.
151. Vermont by far.
152. New Hampshire. Dartmouth College. The University of Vermont must be satisfied with its informal categorization as a "public ivy."
153. *Yankee* is published in Dublin, New Hampshire.
154. New Hampshire. And we are losing ground! In 1960, for every dollar of income earned by a resident of New Hampshire, a resident of Vermont earned 92 cents. Twenty-four years later in 1984, Vermonters earned 81 cents for every dollar earned across the river.
155. New Hampshire does, on Route 302. (This resort in the White Mountains was the site of an important International Monetary Fund conference in 1944.)
156. Vermont.
157. Vermont.
158. New Hampshire. In 1982 New Hampshire's was 78.3%. Vermont's was 77.7%.
159. New Hampshire by 17 miles.
160. Vermont by plenty. In 1983 Vermont had 133 and New Hampshire had 65. However, most of Vermont's were on probation or parole which means that the states were very close if the measure is of adults actually in jail.
161. New Hampshire. Right across from Orange and Caledonia in Vermont.
162. Vermont.
163. New Hampshire. Lake Winnipesaukee.
164. Vermont, but just by a whisker. Both were above the U.S. average.
165. Vermont.
166. New Hampshire.
167. New Hampshire.
168. Vermont.
169. Vermont. In 1984 Vermont had 84.9 and New Hampshire only 29.7.
170. Vermont and it's not even close. In 1984–85 Vermont legislators got $55 per legislative day, $27.50 for a room (if needed), and $22.50 for meals if renting in Montpelier (but only $18.75 if their residence was in the Montpelier vicinity). In New Hampshire they get $100 a year, $3 a day for up to 15 days, and unlimited mileage.
171. New Hampshire had 842,000; Vermont, only 440,000.
172. New Hampshire.
173. Vermont. In 1984 state and local governments in Vermont received $625 per capita. In New Hampshire the figure was $376.
174. White Mountains. This is the town of Newbury, Vermont, along the Connecticut River (the silver thread on the left across the mead-

ow from the village). The closest mountain in the center of the picture is Black Mountain. The far distant massive mountain on the right is Mount Moosilauke. To the left in the distance are others in the White Mountain range in New Hampshire.

175.

Who was Orville Gibson?

Answer

On New Year's Eve, 1958, Newbury farmer Orville Gibson left his kitchen in the dark of pre-dawn, walked across Route 5 to his barn, opened the door, and stepped inside. He was found three months later miles down river bound hand and foot when the ice went out of the Connecticut River. The Orville Gibson murder case is Vermont's most famous. The national press, *Life* magazine and numerous crime and detective magazines made much of the story. A novel was written, *The Lynching of Orin Newfield*. The *Burlington Free Press* offered a substantial reward for many years, but the crime was never solved.

Mt. Polaski guards Newbury from the west and looks down at the village green and the church-spired streets. The wind still murmurs through the great white pines along the river. The seasons come and go and the rhythm of life continues. But not for Orville Gibson. History has closed around the little village and worn smooth the edge of this dark event. Time will tell, they say. But so far time has had nothing to say about the question of who killed Orville Gibson.

CHAPTER 4

"Wait a Minute!"

Vermont's Weather and Other Natural Disasters

A _____'s tail to the west
Is weather coming at its best
A _____'s tail to the east
Is weather coming at its least

(176. It's a _____ tail.)

They say that Vermonters are a taciturn lot, hard to talk to and not quick to strike up a conversation. Perhaps that is because, while most Americans talk about the weather to start off conversations, in Vermont we find that subject too depressing. Actually, Vermont's weather is okay. It wears on you, true. Yet despite some messy exceptions we are spared the massive disasters that befall people in other states. One thing especially nice about Vermont's weather is David Ludlum's treasure of a book about it called *The Vermont Weather Book*, which provides the documentation for much of the following.

177. The coldest temperature ever recorded in Vermont was

    a. −75 degrees.
    b. −50 degrees.
    c. −40 degrees.
    d. so cold that a fire in a woodlot in Victory froze solid at 8:15 A.M. on February 1, 1916.

178. The highest temperature ever recorded in Vermont was

    a. 98 degrees.
    b. 105 degrees.
    c. 110 degrees.
    d. 112 degrees.

The answers to Chapter 4 begin on page 29.

179. Overall, the coldest town in Vermont is

    a. Bloomfield.
    b. St. Johnsbury.
    c. Newport.
    d. Canaan.

180. In Vermont we like to gather 'round a December fire and describe the deep snows of winter that used to fall "back home when we were kids." The 4 snowiest winters in a row recorded in the last century and a half were

    a. 1968–69 through 1971–72.
    b. 1946–47 through 1949–50.
    c. 1918–19 through 1921–22.
    d. 1886–87 through 1889–90.

181. Has any governor ever declared Vermont a "disaster area" because of a snowfall?

    a. Yes
    b. No

182. Newcomers to Vermont that have lived here since 1977 can already brag that they have lived through

    a. the bitterest-cold Christmas Day.
    b. the 2nd coldest February.
    c. the 4th and 5th coldest Januaries recorded in Vermont in the last 100 years.
    d. all of the above.

183. The Great Hurricane of 1938 was especially severe in which region of Vermont?

    a. The Winooski Valley.
    b. The Lake Champlain Islands.
    c. The Lower Connecticut River Valley.
    d. The Northeast Kingdom.

On the following page is a series of 6 questions. Pick the correct answer from the list below. A month may be used more than once.

a. April	e. January
b. August	f. July
c. December	g. November
d. February	h. September

184. The coldest month of the year is   _____

185. The wettest month of the year is   _____

186. The warmest month of the year is   _____

187. The driest month of the year is   _____

188. The month of the year with the temperature closest
to the yearly average is   _____

189. The month of the year in which the temperature
drops the most from the previous month is   _____

190. Between 1895 and 1984 the average temperature in Vermont was

    a. about freezing.
    b. about 10 degrees above freezing.
    c. about 20 degrees above freezing.
    d. none of your damn business.

191. The coldest temperature ever recorded in New England since the
Weather Bureau began keeping coordinated records was recorded in
Vermont.

    a. True
    b. False

192. Vermonters share a fatalism about the weather. They get nervous
when it's nice in the winter and keep looking apprehensively at the
heavens knowing that sometime soon they'll "pay" for it. According to David Ludlum, the greatest debt paid in this century
occurred in Bennington on _____ 14, 1943, when the
temperature _____ overnight.

    a. January, fell from +60 to –12 (72 degrees)
    b. January, fell from +40 to –30 (70 degrees)
    c. February, fell from +45 to –32 (77 degrees)
    d. December, fell from +35 to –35 (70 degrees)

193. When it reached its deepest point, how deep was the snow on top of
Mt. Mansfield during the winter of 1985–86?

    a. 60 inches
    b. 82 inches
    c. 120 inches
    d. 162 inches

194. In 1985 Governor Kunin called a "state of emergency" in Vermont in preparation for Hurricane Gloria. How many people died in Vermont during this storm?

    a. none
    b. 2
    c. 11
    d. 25

195. On the darkest day of the year, we get about _____ fewer hours of sunlight in Vermont than on the brightest day of the year.

    a. 2.5
    b. 4.5
    c. 6.5
    d. 8.5

196. The worst weather in Vermont's history occurred in 1816. We call this year "eighteen hundred and _____ _____ _____."

197. Lake Champlain usually freezes over toward

    a. the end of December.
    b. the end of January.
    c. the end of February.

198. The state has experienced many floods but the most devastating and costly one in the last century was the Great Flood of

    a. 1895.
    b. 1927.
    c. 1952.
    d. 1976.

199. Vermonters are no strangers to snowstorms. Especially those living in Readsboro who, in 3 days of March 1947, experienced the deepest snowstorm of modern times. They recorded a total accumulation of

    a. 3 feet 2 inches.
    b. 4 feet 2 inches.
    c. 5 feet 2 inches.

200. In 1944, Burlington endured 16 consecutive days of temperatures 90 degrees or above.

    a. True
    b. False

201. On November 13, 1833, residents of some Vermont communities witnessed a/an

   a. total solar eclipse.
   b. exhibition of Aurora Borealis.
   c. shower of polluted hailstones.
   d. exceptional meteor shower.

202. Since 1953, there have been _____ tornadoes reported in Vermont.

   a. 18
   b. 35
   c. 60
   d. 110

203. Over 200 people died in the Great Flood referred to in Question #198.

   a. True
   b. False

204. They say in Vermont that if you don't like the weather, wait a minute. Actually, the greatest ranges in temperature occur in the month of

   a. March.
   b. June.
   c. September.
   d. December.

205. Of the following places, which is the wettest?

   a. Bellows Falls (Windham County)
   b. Burke (Caledonia County)
   c. Enosburg (Franklin County)
   d. Peru (Bennington County)

206. According to the official records, it has never been 70 degrees anywhere in Vermont in February.

   a. True
   b. False

Complete this Vermont proverb: When the wind's in the (207.) _____, the sap flows (208.) _____.

Answers:
"Wait a Minute!"

176. cow's
177. b. –50
178. b. 105
179. Bloomfield by far! This Northeast Kingdom town which has a population of only 188 (now we know why!) holds 6 of the 12 all-time low monthly temperature recordings. January 14, 1914: –44; March 8, 1913: –36; April 1, 1923: –12; May 3, 1946: +14; December 30, 1933: –50. The December reading is the coldest ever recorded in Vermont.
180. a. 1968–69 through 1971–72.
181. a. Yes, Gov. Deane Davis did in 1969.
182. d. all of the above.
183. c. The Lower Connecticut River Valley
184. e. January
185. b. August
186. f. July
187. d. February
188. a. April. T.S. Eliot was right, "April is the cruelest month."
189. c. December. (We said you *may* use a month more than once. We didn't say you *had* to.)
190. b. Actually it was 43 degrees. Not so hot.
191. a. True
192. c. February, fell from +45 to –32 (77 degrees)
193. b. 82 inches, which was low—usually it is between 8 and 10 feet.
194. a. none
195. c. 6.5
196. "eighteen hundred and *froze to death*."
197. b. the end of January.
198. b. 1927.
199. b. 4 feet 2 inches (together with snow already on the ground, Readsboro then had a total of 80 inches of snow cover).
200. b. False. This heat wave only lasted 8 consecutive days.
201. d. An exceptional meteor shower. Thousands of shooting stars streaked across the sky each hour. (A total solar eclipse occurred in 1806 and 1932, the Aurora Borealis in 1837, and hailstones possibly polluted from the smokestacks of a coke company in Troy, New York, in June 1950.)
202. a. 18

203. b. False. 84 people died, which is the highest toll from a natural disaster in the state's history.
204. d. December.
205. d. Peru in Bennington County with an average of 50.83 inches of precipitation per year between 1951 and 1980.
206. a. True
207. west
208. best

Which dam is which?

209. _____ The East Barre Dam
210. _____ The Townshend Dam
211. _____ The Union Village Dam

Answer

209. c. The East Barre Dam
210. a. The Townshend Dam
211. b. The Union Village Dam

A

B

C

THE VERMONT INVENTORS PAGE

Match the inventor with the invention or discovery he is known for:

_____ 212. Thomas Davenport (Brandon) 1837   a. globe
_____ 213. Thaddeus Fairbanks (St. Johnsbury) 1830 b. electric motor
_____ 214. Silas Hawes (Shaftsbury) 1814   c. platform scale
_____ 215. James Wilson (Bradford) 1799   d. steel carpenter's square

216. Gardner Colton of Georgia, Vermont, was the first to discover

    a. maple sugar.
    b. seltzer water.
    c. laughing gas.
    d. phosphate fertilizer.

217. The nation's first marble-cutting saw was invented in 1837 by

    a. Thaddeus Grant of Proctor.
    b. Hiram Kimball of Stockbridge.
    c. Henry Bennett of Barre.
    d. William Parkington of Bellows Falls.

218. Julio Buel of Castleton invented the first

    a. turret lathe.
    b. sandpaper.
    c. spoon fishing lure.
    d. rotary pump.

219. Joel A. Ellis of Springfield has been credited as the inventor of American

    a. toy carts.
    b. violin cases.
    c. jointed dolls.
    d. all of the above.

220. Fourteen years before Fulton ran the *Clermont* up the Hudson, Vermonter Samuel Morey ran a paddlewheel steamboat on the Connecticut River.

The answers to this section begin on page 34.

a. True
b. False

221. John M. Weeks of Salisbury invented

    a. the first beehive that didn't kill the bees when honey was taken.
    b. the first egg "grader" that separates white from brown eggs.
    c. the first automated gutter cleaner for dairy barns.
    d. the bunker silo.

222. One of the ships in the famous battle between the Monitor and the Merrimack was built by a Vermonter. Which ship?

223. One of the most famous Green Mountain Boys was an inventor. One of his inventions was a corn-crusher. Who was he?

    a. Ethan Allen
    b. Remember Baker
    c. Seth Warner
    d. Peleg Sunderland

224. Identify: Tabitha Babbit

Answers:
The Vermont Inventors Page

212. b. Thomas Davenport invented the electric motor. (He also invented the first electric piano and electric printing press.)
213. c. Thaddeus Fairbanks invented the platform scale. (He also invented the first iron plow and refrigeration method.)
214. d. Silas Hawes invented the steel carpenter's square.
215. a. James Wilson invented the globe. (He later established a globe factory.)
216. c. Laughing gas. Then Horace Wells used it as an anesthetic for pulling teeth in 1844.
217. b. Hiram Kimball of Stockbridge.
218. c. Spoon fishing lure. (The turret lathe was invented by a Springfield man, James Hartness, in 1891; sandpaper was invented by a Springfield man, Isaac Fisher, Jr., in 1834; the rotary pump was invented in the early 1800's by Vermont inventors John Cooper and Asahel Hubbard.)
219. d. all of the above.
220. a. True. Morey's steamboat operated in 1793.
221. a. John M. Weeks invented a beehive that allowed you to extract the honey without killing the bees. He wasn't a real Vermonter since he was born in Connecticut and lived a full year there before coming to Vermont in 1789.
222.   John F. Winslow built the Union's Monitor (the ship that won). He was born in Bennington in 1810.
223. b. Remember Baker
224.   Probably Vermont's first woman inventor. She invented the circular saw but Jeremiah Hale got the credit.

225.

P.T. Barnum once offered a $50,000 reward for the capture of the Lake Champlain Monster now known as "Champ."

a. True
b. False

Answer

a. True

CHAPTER 5

Under the Golden Dome
Vermont's Legislature

The Legislature in Montpelier is the heart of Vermont's democracy. It is called a citizen's legislature and it is known as rowdy and placid, wise and foolish, and hardworking and lazy—depending on who the critics are and whether or not the legislature has done something they like. It has changed over the years, to be sure. But by and large, it still conforms to Charlie Morrissey's description in *Vermont: A History*: "Legislators have no offices. They have no secretaries. Instead a legislator and a visitor will sit on a Victorian sofa in the lobby outside the legislative chamber and talk over their knee caps like neighbors on a porch bench back home."

Here are a series of categories of legislative types found in the House of Representatives in the 1985–86 session. Rank them according to their percentage of the total membership.

Rank	Category
(largest percentage in the House)	
226. _____	a. Lawyers
227. _____	b. Women
228. _____	c. Farmers*
229. _____	d. Native Vermonters
230. _____	e. Democrats
231. _____	f. Over 65**

(smallest percentage in the House)

* including retired farmers
**during the 1986 session

The answers to Chapter 5 begin on page 40.

232. How many state senators are there in the legislature?

233. Vermont House members are elected to 2-year terms. How long are the terms of state senators?

234. In the 1985–86 session, over half of Vermont's state senators were born outside Vermont.

a. True
b. False

235. In 1937 there were 248 members of the House of Representatives in Montpelier. How many were Democrats?

a. 39
b. 75
c. 109
d. 140

236. In 1953, when McCarthyism was at its height around the country, former Congressman Charles Plumely saw to it that a bill was introduced into the Vermont legislature that would establish a state board to examine textbooks to decide if they were free of pro-communist ideas. The bill came to the floor and

a. passed 210 to 32.
b. passed 120 to 114.
c. was killed 120 to 114.
d. was killed 202 to 11.

237. Vermont, like Nebraska today, used to have a unicameral legislature.

a. True
b. False

238. How many bills did Madeleine Kunin veto in her first 2 years in office (the 1985–86 session of the legislature)?

a. None
b. 3
c. 15
d. 32

239. In 1985 Eric B. Herzik published an article in the *Western Political Quarterly* in which he "scored" the American states on "political openness." Among other things, this score took into account such items as how easy it is to register and vote, legislative record-

keeping, and "citizen access to legislative procedures." On this ranking of political openness (which ranged from 1 to 18) Minnesota ranked highest (18) and Georgia ranked lowest (1). New Hampshire ranked 16. What did Vermont rank, 10 or 15?

240. Vermont legislator Peter Youngbaer has a strange occupation for a politician. What is it?

    a. Undertaker
    b. Clown
    c. Fortune Teller
    d. Artificial Inseminator

241. How many of the 150 members of the House ran unopposed in the 1984 general election?

    a. 10
    b. 34
    c. 61
    d. 82

242. How many of the 150-member House were freshmen in 1984?

    a. 17
    b. 32
    c. 62
    d. 91

243. What percentage of House incumbents that sought reelection were victorious?

    a. 60%
    b. 71%
    c. 84%

One of the most colorful and (nearly all agree) competent legislators in Vermont was Ernest Earle, nicknamed (244.) _____. One of his occupations was growing and selling (245.) _____ _____ (2 words). He chaired the (246.) _____ & _____ Committee, from whence he fought to keep people from shooting (247.) _____ during deer season.

248. What is the average age of a Vermont state senator?

    a. 44
    b. 53
    c. 60
    d. 71

Can You Label the Chart?

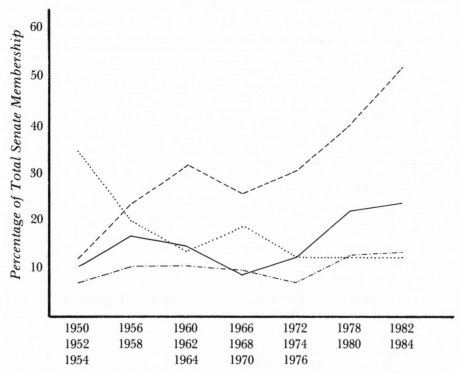

Year of Election

_____	249. _____	a. Percentage of Women
_____	250. _____	b. Percentage of Farmers
··············	251. _____	c. Percentage of Lawyers
_·_·_·_·_·_	252. _____	d. Percentage of Democrats

253. Who was Edna Beard?

    a. The first woman ever elected to the Vermont House.
    b. The first woman ever elected to the Vermont Senate.
    c. a and b.

254. Which of the following did not serve in the Vermont legislature before becoming governor?

    a. Dick Snelling
    b. Deane Davis
    c. Tom Salmon
    d. Philip Hoff

255. How many times have the Democrats held a majority in the Vermont Senate in this century?

    a. 1
    b. 5
    c. 7
    d. 12

256. Who was the last governor of Vermont ever to be elected to the State Senate?

257. Who was the last governor to serve as Speaker of the House of Representatives?

Answers:
Under the Golden Dome

226. d. Native Vermonters (56%)
227. e. Democrats (48%)
228. b. Women (29%)
229. f. Over 65 (27%)
230. c. Farmers (19%)
231. a. Lawyers (3%). Vermont is one of the most "lawyer-free" legisla-
     tures in America.
232. 30
233. They are elected to 2-year terms as well.
234. a. True. Only 13 of the 30 senators are native Vermonters. Six were
     born in Massachusetts, 4 in New York, 2 in Connecticut, and
     one each in Indiana, New Hampshire, New Jersey, Washington,
     D.C., and Switzerland.
235. a. 39. Three were Independents, 2 were Independent Republicans,
     203 were Republicans, and one didn't say. At this time there
     were 89 "pure" farmers and 25 part-time farmers.
236. d. It was killed 202 to 11. Dorothy Canfield Fisher reported the
     reaction of a Vermont newspaper editor who categorized the
     danger of Communists taking over Vermont as follows:
     "Anyone who tries to bore from within in Vermont is going to
     strike granite."
237. a. True
238. b. 3
239. 10. Low, isn't it?
240. b. Clown. (Come to think of it, that might be the perfect vocation
     for a politician.) He is also director of Central Vermont Trans-
     portation. He worked for Clyde Beatty–Cole Brothers Circus.
241. c. 61
242. b. 32
243. c. 84%
244. Stub
245. Christmas trees
246. Fish and Game
247. does
248. b. 53
249. c. Lawyers
250. d. Democrats
251. b. Farmers
252. a. Women

253. c. a and b.
254. b. Deane Davis
255. a. 1
256. Governor Johnson
257. Governor Keyser

258.

In 1942, fifty-nine-year-old Edwine Behre came to Vermont to teach. She returned to Adamant, Vermont, every summer after that. Well into her nineties she continued, as a leading American teacher in her field, to carry on instruction in the tiny village north of Montpelier. What did she teach?

Answer

Piano

Joyce Wolkomir described the beginning of a performance of the Adamant Music School in *Vermont Life's Annual Guide 1978*:

> Nighthawks swoop overhead as the people turn down a side road to an old one-room school with a sign: Adamant Community Club. Inside, chairs scrape as people claim seats. Latecomers cheerfully stand or sit on the floor. Up front, dominating the room like an idol, stands a regal grand piano.
>
> A frail, white-haired lady rises and stands with one tiny hand resting familiarly upon the grand. Her snapping mahogany eyes shine as the people applaud.

CHAPTER 6

Under the River
and Through the Woods
Hunting and Fishing in Vermont

While skiing is Vermont's high-publicity sport, there is an entire strata of Vermont's society that knows outdoor sports in another way. It knows the sharp, chest-tightening cry of a blue jay in a November hard woods at dawn or the urgent snap and tug as your night crawler disappears under a log in the dark swirl of a mountain brook agush with the waters of spring. These are the people that are called by an ancestral longing to reunite with the wild. There are those that point (perhaps rightly) to the unreality of it. But the feeling is real and it helps sustain Vermont's most ardent environmentalists—the outdoor sportspeople. The following are questions from their world.

259. Gerald Stockman of Bradford caught the record brook trout for 1984 in Roaring Brook. It weighed just over

   a. 2 pounds.
   b. 5 pounds.
   c. 9 pounds.

260. It is illegal to hunt bear with dogs in Vermont.

   a. True
   b. False

261. No fishing license is required for ice fishing.

   a. True
   b. False

The answers to Chapter 6 begin on page 53.

262. The two methods of fishing most used in the ice-fishing scene are "tip-ups" and

a. jacks.
b. baiting.
c. jigging.
d. sinking.

263. A person may shoot a black bear at any time in defense of his property.

a. True
b. False

264. Black bears may be taken by gun or bow and arrow but they cannot be taken alive.

a. True
b. False

Match the animal with its track.

Choices

a. Beaver   c. Fox   e. Bear
b. Deer   d. Mink   f. Fisher

265. _____

266. _____

267. _____

268. _____

269. _____

270. _____

271. Open season for moose immediately follows deer season.

    a. True
    b. False

272. It is unlawful to disturb a muskrat house.

    a. True
    b. False

273. The record lake trout taken in Vermont was an even 34 pounds caught in 1981 in Lake

    a. Willoughby.
    b. Champlain.
    c. Morey.
    d. Dunmore.

274. Two of the top 20 bucks shot in 1984 were taken by Buck Noyes and Francis Buck.

    a. True
    b. False

275. Within 20 pounds, give the weight of the biggest buck entered in the 1984 Vermont Big Game Trophy Award Program.

276. One way to positively distinguish different types of trout is by

    a. their length.
    b. their color.
    c. their scales.
    d. their teeth.

277. To be allowed to fish in all parts of the Connecticut River, you need

    a. a Vermont Resident Fishing License.
    b. a New Hampshire Resident Fishing License.
    c. both a and b.
    d. either a or b.

278. The Vermont Fish and Wildlife Department considers the wild turkey to be "Big Game."

    a. True
    b. False

279. A hunter cannot shoot a swimming deer.

   a. True
   b. False

280. How many black bear were taken in the 1985 season in Burlington?

281. For fishing, the legal day begins at

   a. sunrise
   b. midnight.
   c. 6 A.M.
   d. one half hour before sunrise.

282. Scientifically, it's known as Meleagris gallopavo silvestris. The head is naked and a chalky blue. The male has spurs on his legs. What is it?

283. Which of these statements is false?

   a. It is unlawful to leave trash on the ice when ice fishing.
   b. It is unlawful to use a spear gun to take fish.
   c. It is unlawful to set any trap with toothed jaws.
   d. It is unlawful to pick up a deer carcass found on a highway.

284. A "legal" salmon must be at least this long (except in the Willoughby River, and parts of the Barton and Black Rivers).

   a. 15 inches
   b. 20 inches
   c. 25 inches
   d. 30 inches

285. When ice fishing in Lake Champlain, you are allowed to use _____ lines at a time.

   a. 2
   b. 15
   c. 30
   d. any number of

286. "Downriggers" are used in

   a. canoeing.
   b. fishing.
   c. trapping.
   d. bow and arrow hunting.

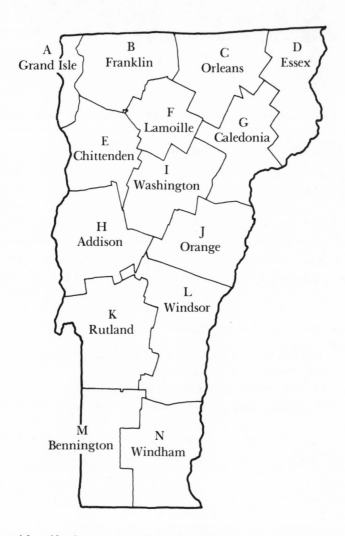

Can you identify the county where in 1985:

_____ 287. The most black bear were killed.

_____ 288. The most wild turkeys were killed.

_____ 289. The second most deer were killed.

_____ 290. The fewest deer were killed.

_____ 291. The fewest bear were killed (excluding Grand Isle County).

_____ 292. The second most turkeys were taken.

_____ 293. The best deer on Vermont's all-time trophy list was shot.

_____ 294. The most wild geese were shot.

295. It's deer season. You shoot a deer legally. Now you must report it. And you must do so within

   a. 1 hour.
   b. 8 hours.
   c. 24 hours.
   d. 48 hours.

296. There is a federal fine of $10,000 for killing an eastern mountain lion in Vermont.

   a. True
   b. False

297. Measured in total pounds taken, which fish is the most important food fish in Vermont?

   a. Brook Trout
   b. Walleyed Pike
   c. Yellow Perch
   d. Smelt

298. The first hunting season for wild turkey in Vermont in modern times was opened in

   a. 1953.
   b. 1963.
   c. 1973.
   d. 1983.

299. As a landowner, you may not ask a hunter to leave your land unless you have posted "No Trespassing" signs.

   a. True
   b. False

300. It is not illegal to shoot the Vermont state bird.

   a. True
   b. False

301. There are approximately 1,500 of them in the state of Vermont. What are they?

   a. Moose
   b. Bobcats
   c. Coyotes
   d. Black Bears

302. A common phrase is "as busy as a beaver." A more appropriate one might be "as precise as a beaver." Not only are beavers capable of cutting down trees but they can fell them precisely where they want.

a. True
b. False

303. A newborn black bear weighs about

a. 3 ounces.
b. 3 pounds.
c. 10 pounds.
d. 30 pounds.

304. It is legal to camp overnight on a roadside or public highway turnout during deer-hunting season.

a. True
b. False

305. There were more antlerless deer than bucks reported killed by hunters in 1985.

a. True
b. False

306. In 1984 a new state record brown trout was taken by Martin Plambeck of East Charleston on the Connecticut River. It weighed

a. 10 pounds 6 ounces.
b. 15 pounds 8 ounces.
c. 25 pounds 10 ounces.

307. The total value of prizes given out in the 1985 Lake Champlain International Fishing Derby was

a. $25,000.
b. $100,000.
c. $250,000.

The following are weights of all-time record fish taken in Vermont through 1984. Match the weight with the fish caught.

308. _____ Chain Pickerel   a. 2 pounds 2 ounces.
309. _____ Northern Pike   b. 8 pounds 4 ounces.
310. _____ Yellow Perch   c. 6 pounds 4 ounces.
311. _____ Largemouth Bass   d. 30 pounds 8 ounces.
312. _____ Walleyed Pike   e. 12 pounds 8 ounces.

313. According to the Fish and Wildlife Department, the largest carp ever taken in Vermont was "landed" by Douglas Bushey of Swanton. He used

a. a 12-gauge shotgun.
b. a bow and arrow.
c. a spear.
d. a fish pole.

314. You are driving along a country road in January and observe a snowmobiler chasing a struggling deer through the deep snow. Is this action illegal?

a. Yes
b. No

315. The Fish and Wildlife Department distributes a flyer defending the use of leg-hold traps. In it they cite, as evidence that leg-hold traps are not all that inhumane, a study by the Ontario Department of Lands and Forests: "Of 805 leg-hold land sets, about _____ showed evidence of any struggle."

a. 5%
b. 20%
c. 35%
d. 50%

316. The bear kill in Vermont dropped _____ between 1984 and 1985.

a. 17%
b. 47%
c. 67%

Rank the following animals according to the number which lost their coats to trappers in Vermont between 1980 and 1984.

Rank *(highest number killed)*	*Animal*
317. _____	a. Beaver
318. _____	b. Bobcat
319. _____	c. Mink
320. _____	d. Raccoon
321. _____	e. Red Fox
322. _____	f. Weasel

(lowest number killed)

323. The first closed season on white-tailed deer (from January 10 to June 10) was established in the year 1825.

   a. True
   b. False

324. In the late 1700's in Bennington it was voted that for "any
    _____ that is killed in Bennington, the person shall be
    paid two coppers, the person bringing in the tail."

   a. bobcat
   b. rattlesnake
   c. panther
   d. wolf

325. Sport fishing alone contributes _____ to Vermont's
    economy each year.

   a. $6 million
   b. $25 million
   c. $75 million

326. The bounty on porcupine was dropped in 1954.

   a. True
   b. False

327. It is permissible to shoot and keep a 50-pound doe in Vermont's
    deer season.

   a. True
   b. False

328. If you are using a Rhode Island Red Hackle, you are

   a. hunting wild geese.
   b. crow hunting.
   c. trout fishing for brookies.
   d. calling wild turkeys.

329. In Manchester, Vermont, there is something that should appeal to
    Vermonters interested in fishing. What is it?

   a. A fly fishing museum.
   b. A fish hatchery.
   c. A manufacturer of specially designed fishing canoes.
   d. The largest stuffed horn pout in existence.

330. In the Fish and Wildlife Department's list of trophy gobblers shot in 1985 (appearing in the June 1986 issue of the *Vermont Sportsman*), the heaviest bird shot was by John Phelps. He got it in Grand Isle and it weighed

    a. 19 pounds 8 ounces.
    b. 24 pounds 0 ounces.
    c. 27 pounds 0 ounces.

331. Which of the following has never been commissioner of the Fish and Wildlife (formerly "Game") Department?

    a. Gary W. Moore
    b. Norman Wright
    c. Brendan Whittaker
    d. Edward Kehoe

332. If you bag one deer (buck or doe) in bow and arrow or in the traditional "gun" season, you may not shoot a buck during Vermont's new muzzleloader deer season.

    a. True
    b. False

333. The Fish and Wildlife Department has referred to not killing enough deer every year as "undergunning."

    a. True
    b. False

334. A popular writer for the *Burlington Free Press*, he is a strong defender of the Vermont Fish and Wildlife Department, especially on the matter of scientific management of the deer herd. His name is?

335. You are in the woods in Vermont and you come upon an orange, diamond-shaped sign, 9 inches wide and 12 inches high, with a black directional arrow on it. What is it?

336. There is no limit on the number of _____ you may trap in a single season in Vermont.

    a. otter
    b. mink
    c. muskrat
    d. all of the above

337. It is unlawful to

  a. use a crossbow for hunting.
  b. use an electronic device to call wild ducks.
  c. both a and b.
  d. neither a nor b.

Answers:
Under the River and Through the Woods

259. b. 5 pounds 4 ounces.
260. b. False
261. b. False
262. c. Jigging is great for catching perch and smelt.
263. a. True
264. a. True. Who wants a pet bear anyway?
265. b. Deer
266. c. Fox
267. e. Bear
268. f. Fisher
269. a. Beaver
270. d. Mink
271. b. False. In Vermont there is no open season for moose, elk, or caribou.
272. a. True
273. a. Lake Willoughby. Caught by a New Hampshire man, John Staples.
274. a. True. We wouldn't fool you, Buckaroo.
275. Randall Moran got a 245-pounder in Bloomfield.
276. d. Vomerine teeth are different in each type of fish.
277. d. Either will work, but a nonresident license is not valid beyond the low-water mark on the Vermont side of the river.
278. a. True
279. a. True, although they might make an exception if it's swimming in your Jacuzzi.
280. None, of course.
281. b. midnight.
282. The wild turkey.
283. None. They are all true.
284. a. 15 inches
285. b. 15 lines (2 hooks per line allowed).
286. b. fishing. (Downriggers are used to deliver fishing lines to desired locations.)
287. d. Essex County
288. k. Rutland County
289. l. Windsor County
290. a. Grand Isle County
291. j. Orange County
292. m. Bennington County

293. i. Washington County
294. h. Addison County
295. d. You must go to a "deer-reporting station" within 48 hours.
296. a. True.
297. c. Yellow Perch
298. c. 1973.
299. b. A landowner can demand a person leave the land whether it is posted or not.
300. b. False.
301. c. Coyotes
302 b. False. Their trees fall randomly and some beavers even miscalculate so badly that they are crushed under the falling tree.
303. a. Only a few ounces.
304. b. It is never legal to camp out on a roadside turnout. And in deer season it is also very dangerous. Especially if you get up early and yawn like a deer.
305. b. False. Bucks—7,494. Antlerless—5,656.
306. b. 15 pounds 8 ounces.
307. c. over $250,000.
308. c. Chain Pickerel—6 pounds 4 ounces.
309. d. Northern Pike—30 pounds 8 ounces. (Bernard Golob got it at Glenn Lake.)
310. a. Yellow Perch—2 pounds 2 ounces.
311. b. Largemouth Bass—8 pounds 4 ounces.
312. e. Walleyed Pike—12 pounds 8 ounces.
313. b. a bow and arrow.
314. a. Yes
315. a. The answer is 5%. This means that 95 out of 100 critters caught by the leg in a steel-jawed trap simply gritted their teeth and hunkered down until clubbed to death by the trapper. We doubt it guys. For starters, all of the woodchucks or porcupines or muskrats we ever trapped (not a whole lot to be sure) struggled *a lot*. Read my lips. 100% of them.
316. b. 47%
317. d. Raccoon (34,770)
318. a. Beaver (7,232)
319. e. Red Fox (6,459)
320. c. Mink (3,146)
321. b. Bobcat (182)
322. f. Weasel (32)
323. b. False. It was established in 1779.
324. b. rattlesnake. Charlotte McCartney reported in the *Vermont History News* that "Windsor County farms were so infested [with

rattlesnakes] until the turn of the century that many hired men walked off their jobs."

325. c. $75 million. The study done by Alphonse Gilbert at the University of Vermont analyzes such items as expenditures for food, lodging, fishing tackle, boats, bait, gasoline, and vehicles.

326. a. True

327. a. True. There is no limit on the size of deer taken. Shooting fawns is permissible, though highly unlikely since deer have their young in the early spring.

328. c. trout fishing for brookies.

329. a. The Museum of American Fly Fishing

330. b. 24 pounds 0 ounces.

331. c. Brendan Whittaker

332. b. False. You can. The bill establishing a muzzleloader season provided: "A person shall not take more than two deer in a calendar year." That means you can't "harvest" three deer in one season—one each with bow, rifle, and muzzleloader.

333. a. True. As God is our witness, *true.*

334. Bish Bishop, one of Vermont's most knowledgeable sportsmen.

335. It's an approved snowmobile directional sign as designated by the Vermont Department of Public Safety under the provisions of Title 31, USA Section 808.

336. d. all of the above.

337. c. both a and b.

338.

Is there a zoo in Vermont?

Answer

No. Although some say there is one in Montpelier that is open during the winter, and that usually closes in late April. Not counting places like Benson's Wild Animal Park in Hudson, N.H., Rhode Island and Connecticut are the only New England states with zoos.

CHAPTER 7

Nice States Finish First

Is it pride or is it self-defense when Vermonters bristle up and proclaim: "But did you know Vermont is the first state that . . . ?" One can imagine the flatlander's inner thoughts: "In New York we have so many firsts we lost count in 1832." Anyway, for a state with a population about the size of Syracuse, New York, we think Vermont does pretty well. Besides, if what our publishers tell us is true, Vermont is the only state in the union to have a decent (339.) _____ book written exclusively for it!

340. Vermont was the first state to join the Union after the original thirteen.

   a. True
   b. False

341. The first shot fired in the War of 1812 was fired in Vermont.

   a. True
   b. False

342. The first canal in the country was built in 1802 in

   a. Bellows Falls.
   b. White River Junction.
   c. Isle La Motte.
   d. Winooski.

The answers to Chapter 7 begin on page 65.

56

343. The first female lieutenant governor ever elected in the United States was elected in Vermont.

    a. True
    b. False

344. The nation's first ski tow was located in

    a. Killington.
    b. Stowe.
    c. Woodstock.
    d. Burke.

345. Norwich University, the nation's first private military school, was originally established in _____ and later moved to _____.

    a. Northfield, Norwich
    b. Newbury, Northfield
    c. Putney, Norwich
    d. Norwich, Northfield

346. The Dresdan School District was the first school district in the U.S. to unite towns on opposite sides of a state boundary. The towns are

    a. Stamford, Vt. and Williamstown, Mass.
    b. Lunenburg, Vt. and Lancaster, N.H.
    c. Alburg, Vt. and Rouses Point, N.Y.
    d. Norwich, Vt. and Hanover, N.H.

347. The first normal school in America was founded in _____, Vermont, in 1823.

    a. Newbury
    b. Wilmington
    c. Fletcher
    d. Concord

348. The first American patent, signed by George Washington, was issued in 1790 to a Vermonter for

    a. potash.
    b. an apple cider press.
    c. chewing tobacco.
    d. ox yokes.

349. Bethel and Randolph were the first towns in America to share a town manager.

a. True
b. False

350. The first alpine slide in North America (which is also the longest) is at what ski area?

a. Stowe
b. Killington
c. Bromley
d. Ascutney

351. The steamboat *Vermont* was the first steamboat to begin commercial service on any of the country's lakes.

a. True
b. False

352. "Snowflake" Bentley of Jericho was the first person to photograph snowflakes, and his studies conclude that no two are alike. Snowflake's first name was really

a. Calvin.
b. William.
c. Hiram.
d. Wilson.

353. Vermont was the first state to allow women to vote.

a. True
b. False

354. Vermont was the first state to adopt universal manhood suffrage.

a. True
b. False

355. A Vermonter was the first person ever to cross the United States by automobile.

a. True
b. False

356. The nation's first marble quarry was started at

a. East Dorset by Isaac Underhill.
b. Proctor by Redfield Proctor.
c. Isle La Motte by Henry Ripley.
d. East Barre by John Judd.

357. Scottish immigrant William F. Milne organized the first
_____ in 1909 while living in Barre.

    a. educational society
    b. Boy Scout Club
    c. museum
    d. labor union

358. Sen. Warren Austin of Burlington, Vermont, was America's first
_____.

359. On one particular January 31, Ida M. Fuller of Ludlow received
$22.54. On that day she became America's first

    a. lottery winner.
    b. recipient of Social Security.
    c. woman to earn money as a politician.
    d. beneficiary of a life insurance policy.

360. The nation's first school of higher education for women was established in

    a. Bennington.
    b. Burlington.
    c. Middlebury.
    d. Rutland.

361. Vermont's constitution was the first state constitution to outlaw slavery.

    a. True
    b. False

362. It was in Vermont that the first black in America

    a. received a college degree.
    b. became a state legislator.
    c. received an honorary college degree.
    d. all of the above.

363. The first _____ _____ (two words) used in
America was made in Brattleboro in 1846.

364. In 1896 Vermont passed the first law that would allow you to carry
your politics with you. What was it?

365. Which of the following is a federal program first used in Vermont?

a. Head Start
b. Civilian Conservation Corps
c. CETA
d. FDIC

366. Which of the following is *not* a Vermont first?

a. The first tri-town water district in the nation.
b. The first death caused by a snowmobile accident in the nation.
c. The first woman admitted to practice law before the Supreme Court.
d. The first French Catholic parish in America.

367. Vermont was the first state to create a state publicity service to promote tourism.

a. True
b. False

368. Vermont was the first state in which a commercial pet cemetery was established.

a. True
b. False

369. The first comedy to be professionally staged in America was written by a man who lived in Vermont.

a. True
b. False

Once in a great while Vermont comes in second. We did so on three of the items listed below. Which three?

370. _____

371. _____

372. _____

a. Having a teacher use a blackboard in class.
b. Establishing a compulsory school-attendance law.
c. Electing a woman speaker of the state's House of Representatives.
d. Having a teacher write a manual on how to teach.
e. Banning the use of corporal punishment in the classroom.
f. Permitting the addition of kindergartens in local school districts.

60

373. In 1985 a college in Putney opened as the country's first college specifically for

   a. fiddle music and contra dancing.
   b. paralyzed students.
   c. equestrian studies.
   d. dyslexic students.

374. Henry Cushman of Bennington is credited with having been the first to use the

   a. rubber eraser.
   b. time clock.
   c. stopwatch.
   d. ballpoint pen.

375. In 1971 Vermont became the first state in the nation to bestow full adult responsibilities and privileges on eighteen-year-olds.

   a. True
   b. False

376. The first known spy to defect to the Soviet Union after World War II was a Vermonter from the village of Moscow.

   a. True
   b. False

Four of the following firsts are Vermont's; four are Alabama's. Which are which?

	Vermont	Alabama
377. First state anti-trust law.	_____	_____
378. First woman secretary of a national political party.	_____	_____
379. First seeding machine patent issued.	_____	_____
380. First air traffic regulation course offered.	_____	_____
381. First meteorite to strike a woman.	_____	_____
382. First anti-sit-down strike legislation.	_____	_____

383. First state-wide, state-supported
educational television
network.   _____   _____

384. First steam-heated factory.   _____   _____

385. Vermont was the first state to have a state symphony orchestra.

    a. True
    b. False

386. Vermont was the first state to outlaw capital punishment.

    a. True
    b. False

When Vermont was settled, often the *first* order of business was the building of a church. Often, too, that church was a Congregational Church—the *First* Congregational Church. Indeed, Congregationalism has been called Vermont's "state" (note the small "s") religion. In any event, whatever they are called today and whoever worships in them, there are some mighty pretty Congregational churches around Vermont. Can you name the town in which the four on the following pages are located?

Your Options:

    a. St. Johnsbury
    b. Marlboro
    c. Middlebury
    d. Westmore

387. _____

388. _____

389. _____

390. _____

Answers:
Nice States Finish First

339. quiz
340. a. True
341. b. False
342. a. Bellows Falls.
343. a. True. Consuelo N. Bailey was elected in 1954.
344. c. Woodstock.
345. d. Norwich, Northfield. Established in 1819, it offered the first civil engineering course.
346. d. Norwich and Hanover.
347. d. Concord
348. a. potash. It's a granular substance created from wood ashes and used in making soap. First made by Samuel Hopkins.
349. b. False, although they were the first towns in Vermont to do so.
350. c. Bromley Ski Area
351. a. True
352. d. Wilson.
353. b. False
354. a. True
355. a. True. Burlington physician H. Nelson Jackson started out from San Francisco in 1903.
356. a. East Dorset by Isaac Underhill in 1785.
357. b. Boy Scout Club
358. ambassador to the United Nations.
359. b. Ms. Fuller received check number 00–000–001 in 1940 for Social Security benefits.
360. c. Established by Emma Willard in Middlebury in 1814.
361. a. True
362. d. all of the above.
363. postage stamp
364. An absentee voting law
365. a. Head Start began in East Fairfield.
366. b. The first death caused by a snowmobile accident.
367. a. True. The first advertisement used to promote Vermont was entitled: "Vermont, Designed by the Creator for the Playground of the Continent."
368. b. False
369. a. True. Royall Tyler wrote *The Contrast* in 1787. Today the Royall Tyler Theater at the University of Vermont offers Vermonters a variety of theatrical entertainment.

370. b. Establishing a compulsory school-attendance law.
371. c. Electing a woman speaker of the House of Representatives.
372. f. Permitting the addition of kindergartens in local school districts. We were *first* in using blackboards and writing a teachers' manual. S.R. Hall did both in Concord.
373. d. dyslexic students (Landmark College).
374. a. rubber eraser.
375. b. False
376. b. Sure, and the Pope's Italian.
377. Alabama in 1883.
378. Alabama.
379. Vermont: to Eliakim Spooner in 1799.
380. Vermont: at Norwich, 1934.
381. In Sylacauga, Alabama (honest!).
382. Vermont in 1937.
383. Alabama on August 9, 1956.
384. Vermont: at the Burlington Woolen Company in 1846.
385. a. True
386. b. False
387. c. Middlebury Congregational Church
388. a. North Congregational Church and United Church of Christ, St. Johnsbury
389. b. Marlboro Meeting House and Congregational Church of Christ
390. d. Westmore Congregational Community Church

391.

In 1961 Robert Frost was named Poet Laureate of Vermont. He was born in 1974. Where?

a. Vermont
b. New Hampshire
c. Massachusetts
d. California

Answer

d. Robert Frost was born in California.

CHAPTER 8

Vermont's People

A civilization is a combination of place and people. Much is made of the current mixture of "native" and "flatlander," but both groups drink the same water, breathe the same air, curse the same weather, and feel the same twinge in their souls when the high pastures flame gold in October. We agree with Peter Jennison and Christina Tree who say, in their excellent source book *Vermont: An Explorer's Guide*, "This stage in Vermont's history [the current period] is as much worth noting as its 14 years as an independent republic." The following questions deal with the sociology of Vermont in the 1980's and its relationship to the past.

392. In 1980 there were more women than men in Vermont.

    a. True
    b. False

393. Between 1980 and 1984 the Vermont population

    a. declined by 1.3%.
    b. grew by 3.6%.
    c. grew by 9.2%.
    d. grew by 17.8%.

394. In which census year was Vermont reported to be the most "urban"? Urban is defined as the percentage of the population living in places of 2,500 or more.

The answers to Chapter 8 begin on page 73.

a. 1910
b. 1940
c. 1960
d. 1980

395. In which decade did Vermont's total population grow the fastest?

a. 1800–1810
b. 1870–1880
c. 1910–1920
d. 1970–1980

396. According to the 1980 Census, there are about how many blacks living in Vermont?

a. 500
b. 1,000
c. 4,000
d. 8,000

397. There were 10 times as many white collar workers as there were farmers and foresters combined in Vermont in 1980.

a. True
b. False

398. Which Vermont county has the largest population?

399. Which Vermont county has the highest population density (people per square mile)?

400. According to the Vermont Department of Health, which county will grow in population the fastest between 1980 and the year 2000 based on the rate of growth between 1970 and 1980?

a. Orange
b. Chittenden
c. Windham
d. Essex

401. In 1980, about how many Abenaki Indians were living in Vermont?

a. 1,500–2,000
b. 5,000–6,000
c. 9,000–10,000

According to the 1980 census, name the county that:

68

_____ 402. grew the second fastest 1970–1980.

_____ 403. had the smallest population.

_____ 404. had the oldest population.

_____ 405. had the lowest median family income.

_____ 406. had the second lowest median family income.

_____ 407. grew the slowest 1970–1980.

_____ 408. had the second lowest percentage of high-school graduates.

_____ 409. had the second highest percentage of women in the work force.

_____ 410. had the second largest population.

_____ 411. after Windham and Windsor had the lowest percentage of Vermont-born residents.

_____ 412. had the highest percentage employment in service industries.

_____ 413. had the youngest population.

_____ 414. does not rank distinctively in any of these kinds of statistics.

_____ 415. had the second highest percentage employed in agriculture.

Rank the following according to the percentage of women in the total membership in 1983.

Rank
(highest percentage)

416. _____

417. _____

418. _____

419. _____

420. _____

421. _____

(lowest percentage)

a. Percentage of women teaching at the 16 colleges in Vermont in 1983.
b. Percentage of town clerks that were women in 1983.
c. Percentage of women serving on boards of directors of banks.
d. Percentage of women judges in 1983 (other than elected assistant judges and probate judges).
e. Percentage of women attorneys.
f. Percentage of women on Vermont's 16 hospital boards.

422. If you were to decide to engage in an Experiment in International Living, you would go to

a. Burlington.
b. Brattleboro.
c. Swanton.
d. Moscow.

70

What Do Vermonters Do?

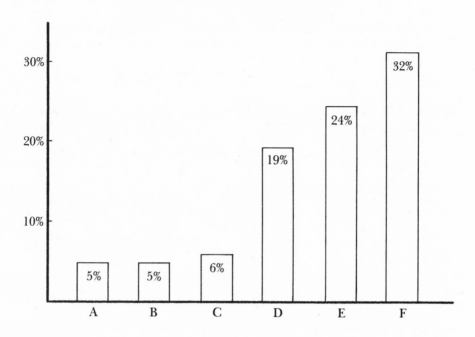

Label the bar chart: Percentage of Vermonters employed in selected industries, 1985:

423. _____ Construction

424. _____ Finance, Insurance, and Real Estate

425. _____ Manufacturing

426. _____ Services

427. _____ Transportation, Communications, and Public Utilities

428. _____ Wholesale and Retail Trade

429. The average number of people receiving food stamps in Vermont in fiscal 1986 was about

   a. 7,000.
   b. 15,000.
   c. 40,000.
   d. 65,000.

Vermonters are a mixed lot. Match the ethnic group with the town or city in which you would be most apt to find them.

_____ 430. Polish   a. Proctor
_____ 431. French   b. Barre
_____ 432. Italians   c. Springfield
_____ 433. Swedes   d. Fairfield
_____ 434. Russians   e. Bellows Falls
_____ 435. Irish   f. Ryegate
_____ 436. Scots   g. Winooski

437. In 1980 what percentage of Vermont's citizens living in the state were actually born here (that is to say, what percentage were "real" Vermonters)?

     a. 44%
     b. 62%
     c. 78%

438. What percentage of Vermont's 210,268 workers working away from home "carpooled" to work in 1980?

     a. 5%
     b. 15%
     c. 26%
     d. 42%

439. How many minutes did it take the average Vermonter to get to work in 1980?

     a. 5 minutes
     b. 10 minutes
     c. 17 minutes
     d. 25 minutes

440. What percentage of all persons over five years old in 1980 in Vermont had moved at least once since 1975?

     a. 16%
     b. 30%
     c. 45%
     d. 62%

Answers:
Vermont's People

392. a. True
393. b. grew by 3.6%.
394. c. 1960. In that year 38.5% of all Vermonters lived in places of 2,500 or more population.
395. a. From 1800 to 1810 Vermont's population grew from 154,465 to 217,895, for a percentage increase of 41.1%. Between 1970 and 1980 we increased at a rate of 15.0%. In the decade between 1910 and 1920 we *lost* population at our highest rate ever, a full 1%, from 355,956 to 352,428.
396. b. At the time of the 1980 Census, there were 1,188. This meant Vermont had the smallest black population in America.
397. a. True. Actually, not quite. There were 11,818 farmers, foresters, and fishermen and 115,510 white-collar workers.
398. Chittenden
399. Chittenden—217 per square mile.
400. a. Orange County
401. a. 1,500–2,000
402. j. Orange. Grand Isle grew the fastest.
403. a. Grand Isle, 4,613.
404. l. Windsor, where the median age was 32.2 years.
405. d. Essex at $12,369.
406. c. Orleans at $14,336.
407. i. Washington
408. b. Franklin. 59.2% of those over 25 had completed high school. In Essex County it was 56.3%.
409. n. Windham
410. k. Rutland
411. m. Bennington
412. f. Lamoille
413. e. Chittenden, where the median age was 26.5.
414. g. Caledonia
415. h. Addison County. Franklin had 11.97%, Addison had 11.69%.
416. b. 80% of town clerks were women in 1983.
417. a. 35% of those teaching at the state's 16 colleges were women.
418. f. 25% of hospital board members were women.
419. e. 9% of attorneys were women in 1983.
420. c. 5% of the people on bank boards were women in 1983.
421. d. 0% women judges. (In 1984 Richard Snelling appointed Linda Levitt to the District Court in Chittenden County.)

422. b. Brattleboro.
423. c. Construction 6%
424. a. Finance, Insurance, and Real Estate 5%
425. e. Manufacturing 24%
426. f. Services 32%
427. b. Transportation, Communications, and Utilities 5%
428. d. Wholesale and Retail Trade 19%
429. c. 40,000.
430. e. Polish, Bellows Falls
431. g. French, Winooski
432. b. Italians, Barre
433. a. Swedes, Proctor
434. c. Russians, Springfield
435. d. Irish, Fairfield
436. f. Scots, Ryegate
437. b. 62% of the population was native-born in 1980.
438. c. 26%
439. c. 17 minutes
440. c. 45%

441.

In 1984, 19% of the members of Vermont's House of Representatives in Montpelier were women. Twenty years earlier in 1964, _____ of the members of that same body were women.

a. 4%
b. 9%
c. 14%
d. 19%

Answer

d. 19% women in the 1964 House.

VERMONT LIFESTYLES
OF THE RICH AND/OR FAMOUS PAGE

The following matching items make sense because of a famous person:

_____ 442. Thetford   a. *The Jungle Book*

_____ 443. Dummerston   b. "Little Boy Blue"

_____ 444. Barnard   c. *Elmer Gantry*

_____ 445. Newfane   d. Wells-Fargo

Match the town with the famous person:

_____ 446. John Kenneth Galbraith   a. Bennington

_____ 447. Grandma Moses   b. Bethel

_____ 448. William Lederer   c. Bradford

_____ 449. Admiral George Dewey   d. Danby

_____ 450. Chief Justice William Rehnquist   e. Greensboro

_____ 451. Helen Gahagan Douglas   f. Island Pond

_____ 452. Pearl Buck   g. Montpelier

_____ 453. Vilhjamur Stefansson   h. Newfane

_____ 454. Rudy Vallee   i. Peacham

_____ 455. Ellsworth Bunker   j. Dummerston

456. Prior to 1985, which person never set foot in Vermont?

     a. Abraham Lincoln
     b. Muhammad Ali
     c. Margaret Whiting*
     d. Mark Twain

457. The Rockefeller family is associated with the town of

_____.

458. One of the most significant writers of the twentieth century lives permanently and year-round in Cavendish, Vermont. His name is

_____.

459. One of America's best-known novelists taught for years at Bennington College. He died in 1986. His name was

_____.

*The singer who popularized "Moonlight in Vermont."

The answers to this section begin on page 77.

Vermont and the Movies

460. Which of the following has the *least* association with Vermont?

    a. Paul Newman
    b. Sylvester Stallone
    c. Robert Redford
    d. Charles Bronson

461. Maria von Trapp, who operates the Trapp Family Lodge in Stowe, reminds us immediately of the movie classic

_____.

462. Which of the following movies was *not* filmed in Vermont?

    a. *The Survivors*
    b. *Ghost Story*
    c. *Downhill Racer*
    d. *The Trouble with Harry*

Perhaps the most famous scene ever filmed in Vermont starred (463.) _____ in the movie (464.) _____. It was filmed on the (465.) _____ River.

Many of Vermont's rich and famous stay here.

466. What is the name of this structure?

467. Where is it located?

Answers:
Vermont Lifestyles of the Rich and/or Famous Page

442. d. Henry Wells of Thetford was the Wells of the Wells-Fargo Company.
443. a. Rudyard Kipling wrote both *Jungle Book* and *Captains Courageous* in Dummerston.
444. c. Sinclair Lewis, author of *Elmer Gantry* and *Babbitt*, called Barnard, Vermont, "one of the few decent places in America to live."
445. b. Eugene Field, who has been called the "poet of American childhood," played on the green in Newfane as a boy.
446. h. John Kenneth Galbraith has a summer house in Newfane.
447. a. The schoolhouse Grandma Moses attended as a child is in Bennington,* where she lived for a time.
448. i. The author of *A Nation of Sheep* lives in Peacham.
449. g. The Admiral of Manila Bay grew up across from the capitol building in Montpelier.**
450. e. Greensboro, Vermont's Caspian Lake is a great gathering point for the rich and famous, including Bernard DeVoto and Justice Rehnquist.
451. c. Helen Gahagan Douglas, target of Richard Nixon and wife of Oscar-winning actor Melvyn Douglas, has a place in Bradford.
452. d. The author of the *Good Earth*, Pearl Buck lived in Danby.
453. b. Polar explorer Vilhjamur Stefansson had a summer home in Bethel.
454. f. Vallee the singer was born in Island Pond. He died in July 1986.
455. j. The late Ellsworth Bunker of Dummerston was U.S. Ambassador to South Vietnam.
456. c. Margaret Whiting visited for the first time in 1985. Abraham Lincoln stayed at the Equinox Inn in Manchester. Muhammad Ali's bus once broke down on I–91 in southern Vermont where he charmed and impressed as a soft-spoken gentleman. Mark Twain not only visited Vermont but left us the following story as told by Charlie Morrissey in *Vermont: A History*: "Samuel Clemens (Mark Twain) discovered the same characteristics [Vermonters are careful not to show their feelings] when he lectured once in Brattleboro and couldn't induce any substantial

*It was moved there from Eagle Bridge, New York.
**Did you confuse him with Burlington's John Dewey, the famous philosopher and educator?

laughter from his audience of stone-faced Vermonters. Wondering why his humor was so ineffectual that night, he walked around to the front of the theater afterwards and heard a Vermonter helping his wife into their buggy say, 'B'golly, that fellow was so funny tonight I could hardly keep from laughing.' "

457. Woodstock
458. Aleksandr Solzhenitsyn
459. Bernard Malamud (author of *A New Life* and *The Natural*).
460. b. Sylvester Stallone. Paul Newman and Joanne Woodward eat often at the Old Tavern in Grafton. The Robert Redfords bought a home on Lake Champlain and Charles Bronson and his wife Jill Ireland live in Brownsville.
461. *The Sound of Music*
462. c. *Downhill Racer*
463. Lillian Gish
464. *Way Down East*
465. White
466. The Equinox Inn
467. Manchester

Rank the Vermont Municipalities
According to Their Size in Population in 1980

Municipality	Rank (1=largest)
468. Barre City	_____
469. Bennington Town*	_____
470. Brattleboro Town	_____
471. Burlington City	_____
472. Colchester Town	_____
473. Essex Town*	_____
474. Montpelier City	_____
475. Rutland City	_____
476. Springfield Town	_____

477. Which of the above municipalities grew the fastest between 1970 and 1980?

478. Which grew the slowest?

Answers

468. Barre City, 8
469. Bennington Town, 3
470. Brattleboro Town, 6
471. Burlington City, 1
472. Colchester Town, 5
473. Essex Town, 4
474. Montpelier City, 9
475. Rutland City, 2
476. Springfield Town, 7
477. Colchester Town grew the fastest at 30.5%.
478. Rutland City actually declined in population by 4.4%. Rutland was followed closely by the state capital, which lost 4.3% of its population between 1970 and 1980.

*Includes villages

CHAPTER 9

D. Y. K. W. T. S. F.
Do You Know What These Stand For?

One phenomenon that consistently amazes visitors to Vermont is the degree to which Vermonters are joiners. The stereotype of the Vermonter as "anti-social" just isn't true. Below is a tiny listing of the abbreviations for Vermont businesses, groups, activities, hobbies, and places with our apologies for the many left unmentioned. Guess what each stands for.

479. SMC _____
Hint: Purple Knights gather here.

480. VAST _____
Hint: You'll only see these folks in the winter.

481. B&B _____
Hint: The basics for travelers.

482. VWPC _____
Hint: You might find Madeleine at one of these.

483. VDMV _____
Hint: It should have a "Drive Thru" section.

484. MCHV _____
Hint: Is your Blue Cross up to date?

The answers to Chapter 9 begin on page 83.

485. St. J   _____
     Hint: A place to go to, not a saint to pray to.

486. RFD   _____
     Hint: Neither rain, nor snow, nor gloom of night.

487. GMC (no relation to General Motors)_____
     Hint: Look for them on the Long Trail.

488. BOV   _____
     Hint: Once it was the BSB.

489. PACE   _____
     Hint: Trinity keeps up the pace!

490. SAVE   _____
     Hint: Hunters care about the environment, too.

491. HFT   _____
     Hint: You can't get your license without it anymore.

492. VPIRG   _____
     Hint: You might take an interest in their activities.

493. VINS   _____
     Hint: Naturally, Vermont would have one.

494. GMP   _____
     Hint: A "powerful" organization.

495. VNA   _____
     Hint: Doctors don't make house calls but they do.

496. GMNF   _____
     Hint: Smokey the Bear's hangout.

497. VT   _____
     Hint: Do you really need a hint?

498. VAPCOO _____
     Hint: Have Winnebago, Will Travel.

499. ELF   _____
     Hint: These workshops don't make toys.

500. VCUG _____

    Hint: Get your **PC**, **LOGON**, and you're in.

501. VHS _____

    Hint: Not a high school but dedicated to the preservation of the story of our state.

502. VEA _____

    Hint: You might belong if you work at U–32.

503. VADA _____

    Hint: *You* don't have to be over 100 to join.

504. VPA _____

    Hint: Gets our *stamp* of approval.

505. CVPS _____

    Hint: "C V & You."

506. DAR _____

    Hint: Nope, you should know this one.

507. FFA _____

    Hint: If we don't watch out, we won't need this one anymore.

508. VAB _____

    Hint: There are many ways to see Vermont.

Answers:
D. Y. K. W. T. S. F.

479. Saint Michael's College
480. Vermont Association of Snow Travelers
481. Bed and Breakfast
482. Vermont Women's Political Caucus
483. Vermont Department of Motor Vehicles
484. Medical Center Hospital of Vermont
485. St. Johnsbury
486. Rural Free Delivery
487. Green Mountain Club
488. Bank of Vermont (originally the Burlington Savings Bank)
489. Program for Adult Continuing Education
490. Sporting Alliance for Vermont's Environment
491. Hunter Firearms Training
492. Vermont Public Interest Research Group
493. Vermont Institute of Natural Science
494. Green Mountain Power
495. Visiting Nurse Association
496. Green Mountain National Forest
497. Vermont
498. Vermont Association of Private Campground Owners and Operators
499. Environmental Learning for the Future (sponsored by VINS)
500. Vermont Computer Users Group
501. Vermont Historical Society
502. Vermont Education Association
503. Vermont Antique Dealers Association
504. Vermont Philatelic Association (stamp collectors)
505. Central Vermont Public Service
506. Daughters of the American Revolution
507. Future Farmers of America
508. Vermont Association of the Blind

509.

What is the vice president saying?

a. "I don't care who he is, arrest him."
b. "And this is my other brother, Daryl."
c. "Gosh, golly gee. Jimmy and I are so happy to be back in Concord—er, is that where we are?"
d. "Remember, Jim, you're a Republican, a Republican, a Republican . . . "
e. We really don't know.

Photo by Joe Mahoney—*Burlington Free Press*

Answer

e. We really don't know.

CHAPTER 10

You Can't Get There from Here
Vermont Roads

Vermonters are proud of their ability to get around the state. Most of all they cherish their capacity to know direction. They delight in taking the short cut, the back road that "brings them out" just a few miles "above" the village or "below" the Carbee farm. Those that are not capable of driving the state on their own are often forced to stop and ask directions. And you know what that means.*

510. You are in Island Pond and you need to get to Lyndon State College. Which road do you take?

    a. Vermont 102
    b. U.S. 5
    c. Vermont 114
    d. U.S. 2

511. I–91 and I–89 intersect in the town of

    a. Norwich.
    b. Hartford.
    c. Windsor.
    d. Sharon.

512. To go from Bentley's Restaurant in Woodstock to Barnard, take

    a. U.S. 4.
    b. Vermont 12.
    c. Vermont 106.
    d. none of the above.

*See the story at the end of the question section.

The answers to Chapter 10 begin on page 93.

513. Which of the following route numbers does not belong on a state highway sign?

  a. 100
  b. 302
  c. 105
  d. 9

514. If you stick to state and/or federal highways, which two locations are the furthest apart?

  a. Springfield and Bellows Falls
  b. Londonderry and Weston
  c. Bradford and Newbury
  d. Burlington and Montpelier

515. Routes 15 and 104 intersect in the town of

  a. Cambridge.
  b. Morrisville.
  c. Manchester.
  d. Rutland.

516. If you are on Route 15 heading east from Jeffersonville to West Danville, which of the following locations is *not* on the way?

  a. Wolcott
  b. Hardwick
  c. Johnson
  d. Elmore
  e. All of the above

517. To get from Brandon to Rochester you take Route

  a. 4.
  b. 7.
  c. 73.
  d. 116.

518. The principal north–south highway in Grand Isle County is

  a. U.S. 2.
  b. Vermont 7.
  c. Vermont 108.
  d. I–91.

519. To get from Guildhall to Island Pond go _____ on Route 102 to

_____ and then _____ on Route _____.

   a. south/Lunenburg/west/2
   b. east/Bloomfield/north/105
   c. north/Bloomfield/west/105
   d. north/Lyndonville/east/114

520. You are traveling south on Route 5A. Soon after Routes 58 and 16 connect from the west, a long lake parallels the highway on your right. What is its name?

   a. Memphremagog
   b. Crystal
   c. Bomoseen
   d. Willoughby

521. Route 9 between Brattleboro and Bennington might also be called

   a. the Bayley–Hazen Military Road.
   b. the Molly Stark Trail.
   c. the Appalachian Trail.
   d. the Long Trail.

Match the highway with its other name:

522. _____ Route 302	a.	Calvin Coolidge Memorial Highway
523. _____ Route 15	b.	Grand Army of the Republic Highway
524. _____ Route 132	c.	Theodore Roosevelt Highway
525. _____ Route 2	d.	William Scott Memorial Highway
526. _____ Route 103	e.	Justin Smith Morrill Highway

"Gaps," "Gorges," and "Gulfs." Match the geological phenomenon with the highway you'd be on as you passed through it.

527. _____ Appalachian Gap	a.	Route 100
528. _____ Granville Gulf	b.	Route 4
529. _____ Quechee Gorge	c.	Route 17
530. _____ Middlebury Gap	d.	Route 14
531. _____ Williamstown Gulf	e.	Route 12
532. _____ Hubbardton Gulf	f.	Route 125
533. _____ Brookfield Gulf	g.	Route 30

534. You are traveling east on Route 302 on your way to the Happy Hour Restaurant in Wells River. When you come to the junction of Route 25, what do you do?

   a. Take 25
   b. Stay on 302
   c. Turn around, you're lost

535. Amtrak's Montrealer from Washington to Montreal makes several stops in Vermont but it does not stop in

   a. Waterbury.
   b. Essex Junction.
   c. Bellows Falls.
   d. Bennington.

536. How many airlines served the state of Vermont in 1986?

   a. 3
   b. 7
   c. 10
   d. 16

Find the route that will take you across Vermont's border into one of our neighboring states or Canada.

537. _____ Canada   a. Vermont 74
538. _____ New Hampshire   b. Vermont 8
539. _____ Massachusetts   c. Vermont 108
540. _____ New York   d. Vermont 25

The first bridge across the Connecticut River was located at (541.) _____ and was built in (542.) _____.

541.   *542.*

a. Bellows Falls   a. 1761
b. Bradford   b. 1785
c. Lunenburg   c. 1810
d. Chester

543. Roads built to bypass toll roads were called

   a. "notolls."
   b. "shunpikes."
   c. "byways."
   d. "getarounds."

544. The Vermont Historical Railroad operates a scenic 13-mile railroad trip which includes the Brockway Mills Gorge between

   a. St. Albans and Sheldon Springs.
   b. Richmond and Waterbury.
   c. Manchester and Arlington.
   d. Chester and Bellows Falls.

545. Heading south on Route 100 towards Weston Village you encounter a 7-mile humpback in the road known as

    a. "Terrible Mountain."
    b. "The Long Climb."
    c. "Rocky Road."
    d. "The 7-Mile Humpback."

546. If you head east from Route 100 in Rochester over the "Bethel Mountain Road" and turn right when you "come out," what town do you end up in?

547. If you head east from Route 16 in Greensboro Bend over the "Stannard Mountain Road" and keep going until you "come out," what town will you be in?

548. Which of the following runs through the Green Mountain National Forest?

    a. Route 4
    b. Route 30
    c. Route 2
    d. Route 5

549. The historic Crown Point Road followed which route?

    a. Route 5 through St. Johnsbury
    b. Route 105 through North Troy
    c. Route 103 through Ludlow
    d. Route 30 through Townshend

550. You're in Harmonyville. You're between

    a. Jamaica and Rawsonville.
    b. Grafton and Chester.
    c. Chester and Springfield.
    d. Newfane and Townshend.

551. According to the "severity index" established by the National Safety Council, the most severe accidents (cost per accident in life, limb, and property damage) in the five years between 1980 and 1984 occurred where?

    a. I–89 in Randolph
    b. Vermont 105 in Newport
    c. Vermont 100 in Wilmington
    d. Vermont 73 in Goshen

552. Irrespective of the amount of traffic, the damage caused, and the length of the section of road considered, where did the *most* accidents occur between 1980 and 1984?

a. U.S. 7 in Rutland City
b. Vermont 15 in Essex
c. U.S. 5 in Brattleboro
d. Vermont 14 in Barre City

553. Which is the most dangerous intersection in terms of the number of accidents that occur there?

a. The intersection of U.S. 5, U.S. 2 (east), and Bay Road in St. Johnsbury.
b. The intersection of U.S. 5, Vermont 14, and U.S. 4 (east) in Hartford.
c. The intersection of U.S. 7 and Strong Avenue in Rutland.
d. The intersection of U.S. 2 and Airport Drive in South Burlington.

554. It is where the towns of Montgomery, Westfield, and Lowell come together. Route 58 goes through it now. A famous military road was the first to use it and there is a marker there commemorating the older highway. It is?

555. If you are driving on Vermont's Skyline Drive, you would be on Mt. _____.

Above is a crossroads in Addison County. It is located in the town of (556.) _____.

Below you are looking at the (557.) _____ River from a bridge on Route 105 at Sheldon Junction as you travel east between St. Albans and Enosburg Falls.

Above is another crossroads in Vermont, in the city of (558.) _____.

Below is a crossroads in the Northeast Kingdom in the town of (559.)
_____.

*Just about the time one thinks they've heard all the "how do you get to" jokes, you run into another. How about this one that appears in Judson Hale's *Inside New England.* We have quoted it word for word from Hale's book:

> Writer Bill Conklin tells a true "asking directions" story that occurred several years ago when he was moving from "away" to the town of Walpole, New Hampshire. He'd somehow wound up across the Connecticut River from Walpole, in the town of Westminster, Vermont, and although he could plainly see the church spires of Walpole, he couldn't find the road to the bridge that would get him there. Finally, he stopped to ask directions. The classic setup.
>
> "Can you tell me how to get across to Walpole?" he asked an elderly gentleman walking along beside the road.
>
> "Well, turn right a few hundred yards down this road, cross the bridge, and you'll be there," the man said in what appeared to be a very un-Vermontlike response to a tourist asking directions.
>
> But then, after a short pause, he added, "I wouldn't go there, though."
>
> "Why shouldn't I?" Bill asked, at once apprehensive.
>
> "Didn't say *you* shouldn't," he replied. "Said *I* wouldn't."

Answers:
You Can't Get There from Here

510. c. Vermont 114
511. b. Hartford.
512. b. Vermont 12.
513. b. 302 is a U.S. highway.
514. d. Burlington and Montpelier
515. a. Cambridge
516. d. Elmore
517. c. 73
518. a. U.S. 2.
519. c. north/Bloomfield/west/105
520. d. Willoughby
521. b. the Molly Stark Trail.
522. d. William Scott Memorial Highway. Private William Scott fell asleep on guard duty during the Civil War. (He had taken a sick friend's shift the night before.) Ordered to be shot by firing squad, he was spared by Abraham Lincoln in a celebrated case. But Scott was never to return to his homeland hills of Groton. He was killed during a charge at Lee's Mill, Virginia.
523. b. Grand Army of the Republic Highway
524. e. Justin Smith Morrill Highway
525. c. Theodore Roosevelt Highway
526. a. Calvin Coolidge Memorial Highway
527. c. Route 17
528. a. Route 100
529. b. Route 4
530. f. Route 125
531. d. Route 14
532. g. Route 30
533. e. Route 12
534. b. Stay on 302
535. d. Bennington.
536. c. 10 airlines: USAIR, United, PeopleExpress, Piedmont, Empire, PBA, Pilgrim, Ransome, Bar Harbor, and Precision (according to *Doing Business in Vermont*, Agency of Development and Community Affairs).
537. c. 108 at Berkshire
538. d. 25 at Bradford
539. b. 8 at Stamford
540. a. 74 at Shoreham

541. a. Bellows Falls. (If you said Chester, you're *really* a flatlander.)
542. b. 1785
543. b. "shunpikes."
544. d. Chester and Bellows Falls.
545. a. "Terrible Mountain."
546. Bethel
547. Nope, not Stannard. You'll be in Lyndon.
548. b. Route 30. (Route 4 abuts the southern border of the northern half of the Green Mountain Forest but doesn't run through it.)
549. c. Route 103 through Ludlow
550. d. Newfane and Townshend.
551. d. Vermont 73 in Goshen. Although there were only 2 accidents here, they were very bad ones. The severity index was 108,480. In comparison, there were 13 accidents on Vermont 100 in Wilmington but the severity index was only 7,220.
552. a. Route 7 in Rutland
553. c. Rutland again. There were 98. a. = 21, b. = 58, d. = 60. Actually, when the amount of traffic is taken into account (the "actual/critical ratio"), the worst intersection in Vermont is at the intersection of Vermont 104 and Vermont 36 in St. Albans Town.
554. Hazen's Notch. The military road was called the Bayley–Hazen. It began in Newbury.
555. Equinox. (Opened in the summer of 1947, Skyline Drive travels to the top of Big Equinox, 3,816 feet above sea level. It is between 6 and 7 miles long.)
556. Brandon. Note the ever-present Civil War Memorial.
557. Missisquoi. In 1984 a Central Vermont train derailed and crashed into and destroyed part of this bridge.
558. St. Albans
559. Brighton. If you said Island Pond, give yourself credit.

560.

In 1949 a famous Vermont politician said the following to a group of Vermonters in Lyndonville: "You know, this is such beautiful country up here. It ought to be called the Northeast Kingdom of Vermont." Who was he?

Answer

George Aiken named the Northeast Kingdom (who else?).

CHAPTER 11

Footprints on Granite

Vermont History

"Contrary Country" is what Ralph Nading Hill calls it. And it was. In an earlier book we described Vermont's view of Vermont's history as follows: "At war with New York, shooting it out with the British, negotiating with Canada, storming Congress to demand admittance into the Union, playing Robin Hood with Albany sheriffs, capturing the largest British fort in America even before the Revolutionary War had begun . . . that is Vermont as Vermonters see it. The exploits continue . . . many true, some myth, all of them feeding a healthy state ego." Accepted truth is to historians what bee trees are to bears—they like to tear them down. But the "accepted truths" of Vermont's past endure like the mountains in which they were born. Indeed, one of the most accurate of the "accepted truths" about Vermont is that we have one of the best cadres of state historians in North America. They are shepherded in part by the Vermont Historical Society,* which is one reason only the truest of the truths remain true: all of them are subject to the incessant bombardment of good ol' Yankee squint-eyed critique. If you score poorly on this chapter, membership in the Vermont Historical Society is your clearest route to redemption.

561. When Samuel de Champlain conducted his famous battle with the Indians, he fought on the side of the Algonquins against the

*Two of their publications, especially, lead our list of "the most helpful sources": *Vermont History News* and *The Green Mountaineer*. The latter is truly a gem and should be found in the home of every Vermonter who has children, knows someone who has a child, or used to be a child.

The answers to Chapter 11 begin on page 106.

a. Mohawks.
b. Penobscots.
c. Mohegans.
d. Iroquois.

562. The first settler in Vermont from New Jersey was

a. Ethan Allen.
b. responsible for paving Vermont's first highway.
c. driven out of Vermont by the Green Mountain Boys in 1781.
d. not determined by the editors of this book.

563. What did George Van Dyke and Dan Bosse have in common and why are they key figures in the history of Vermont?

564. The first governor of Vermont was

a. Thomas Chittenden.
b. Ira Allen.
c. Jacob Bayley.
d. Ethan Allen.

565. The first female governor of Vermont was

a. Betsy Ross.
b. Fanny Allen.
c. Mrs. Mortimer Proctor.
d. Madeleine Kunin.

566. What were the Green Mountain Boys organized to do?

567. Which one of the following was not a Green Mountain Boy?

a. Seth Warner
b. Remember Baker
c. Jacob Bayley
d. Ira Allen

568. Matthew Lyon was elected to Congress from four different states.

a. True
b. False

569. When was the Tunbridge Fair first held?

a. 1867
b. 1901
c. 1948

570. What was the "High Chair Treatment"?

571. A town in Vermont was originally named Wildersburgh. At town meeting, a vote on the substitute names of Holden and _____ ended in a tie. Champions were picked to defend each name. Fisticuffs ensued and a victorious blacksmith won the town the current name of

    a. Montpelier.
    b. Barre.
    c. Bristol.
    d. Ludlow.

572. The only Revolutionary War battle fought entirely on Vermont soil was the Battle of

    a. Bennington.
    b. Hubbardton.
    c. St. Albans.
    d. Strafford.

573. On January 15, 1777, Vermont signed a Declaration of Independence from New York at

    a. Windsor.
    b. Westminster.
    c. Hubbardton.
    d. Dorset.

574. In the 1800's the Georgia Legislature suggested that Irish laborers be hired to dig a ditch around Vermont and float the state out to sea. Why?

    a. Because Vermont favored abolition of slavery.
    b. Because Vermont, following Maine's lead, prohibited liquor.
    c. Because Vermont opposed formation of the Mason–Dixon Line.
    d. None of the above.

575. Who was the American general at the Battle of Bennington?

576. What did Vermonters Charles Paine, Erastus Fairbanks, J. Gregory Smith, and John Page all have in common besides the fact that they all served as governors of the state?

577. The office of the Overseer of the Poor, authorized to disburse funds to needy people in the towns,

a. was abolished in 1850.

b. was abolished in 1904.

c. was abolished in 1972.

d. still exists today in many towns.

578. The *Burlington Free Press* began publication in

a. 1828.

b. 1872.

c. 1910.

d. 1944.

What was the role of each of the following early town officers?

579. Tythingmen

580. Deerrifts

581. Haywards

Match the event with the correct year from the time line.

Time Line

582. _____ First train to run in Vermont.

583. _____ The Great Blizzard.

584. _____ A Democrat was elected to Congress from Vermont.

585. _____ The year of no summer.

586. _____ The last panther was shot.

587. _____ Vermont's first TV station went on the air.

588. _____ First license plate was issued.

589. _____ Vermont joined the Union.

590. _____ First Democrat since the Civil War was elected governor.

591. _____ The Royalton Raid took place.

592. _____ The Republic of Vermont was formed.

593. _____ The Westminster "Massacre."

594. _____ *Vermont Life* was established.

595. _____ The Vermont legislature gave up control of the deer herd.

```
1775
1777
1780
1789
1791
1800
1816
1832
1848
1867
1870
```

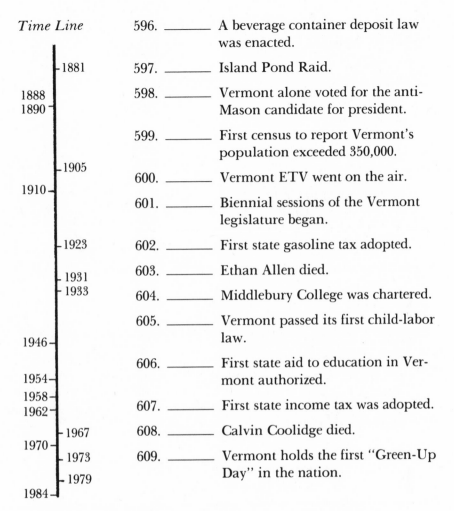

Time Line

1881
1888
1890
1905
1910
1923
1931
1933
1946
1954
1958
1962
1967
1970
1973
1979
1984

596. _____ A beverage container deposit law was enacted.

597. _____ Island Pond Raid.

598. _____ Vermont alone voted for the anti-Mason candidate for president.

599. _____ First census to report Vermont's population exceeded 350,000.

600. _____ Vermont ETV went on the air.

601. _____ Biennial sessions of the Vermont legislature began.

602. _____ First state gasoline tax adopted.

603. _____ Ethan Allen died.

604. _____ Middlebury College was chartered.

605. _____ Vermont passed its first child-labor law.

606. _____ First state aid to education in Vermont authorized.

607. _____ First state income tax was adopted.

608. _____ Calvin Coolidge died.

609. _____ Vermont holds the first "Green-Up Day" in the nation.

610. There were no hospitals in Vermont prior to 1876. The first one established was

a. Mary Fletcher in Burlington.
b. Fanny Allen in Winooski.
c. Putnam Memorial in Bennington.
d. St. Johnsbury Hospital.

611. What was Vermont's first name (two words)?

612. Isaac Eddy, Oliver Tarbell, and George White were three of Vermont's earliest

a. legislators.
b. artists.
c. railroad engineers.
d. commercial maple syrup producers.

613. Vermont coins were first minted in Bennington County in 1785 in the town of

a. Bennington.
b. Dover.
c. Pownal.
d. Rupert.

614. Adopted in 1779, the Vermont State Motto is

a. Liberty and Freedom.
b. Freedom and Unity.
c. Liberty and Unity.
d. Liberty, liberty, liberty, liberty . . . liberty.

615. The first white settlement in Vermont was located in

a. Brattleboro.
b. Vernon.
c. Isle La Motte.
d. Shaftsbury.

616. During the Revolutionary War, the Allen brothers and others secretly negotiated with the British about the possibility of Vermont becoming a British province. We know these infamous excursions into frontier diplomacy as

a. the Allens' Revenge.
b. the Haldimand Negotiations.
c. the Bayley–Hazen Talks.
d. the Allen–Arnold Negotiations.

617. Thomas Chittenden, a man who was governor of Vermont longer than any other person in history, had a physical handicap. What was it?

618. In the 1960's Vermonters were shocked when someone fired at a black minister's home in the Northeast Kingdom. This event became known as _____.

619. The famous pine tree in the Vermont State Seal stood throughout most of Vermont's history. It blew down some years ago in the town of _____.

620. Lt. Gov. S. Hollister Jackson died while driving home on a rainy Montpelier evening in 1927. How did he die?

Which of the following were *not* true when:

621. Calvin Coolidge was president.

    a. Vermont sent two representatives to Congress along with its two senators.

    b. Red clover was the state flower.

    c. The state was losing population.

622. Philip Hoff was governor.

    a. I–91 was not completed.

    b. The Vernon Nuclear Power Plant was under construction.

    c. Act 250 was in effect.

623. Ira Allen was alive.

    a. The Vermont State Senate was in operation.

    b. Montpelier was the state capital.

    c. The state's population was less than 100,000.

624. In 1894 Erastus Baldwin, a harness maker in Wells River, Vermont, built what was called by newspapers of the time the largest _____ in the United States.

    a. waterwheel

    b. delivery wagon

    c. windmill

    d. hot air balloon

625. During the Civil War, Vermonters (commanded by Gen. George J. Stannard of St. Albans) were credited with making one of the most decisive and significant military maneuvers of the war. What was it?

626. What was the "Ely War"?

The (627.) _____ Tavern, headquarters of the Green Mountain Boys, is located in (628.) _____.

627.	628.
a. Flowing Bowl	a. Bennington
b. King George	b. Killington
c. Catamount	c. Shaftsbury
d. Killington	d. Panton

629. Who was Seth Hubbell?

630. We have had four different governors named Smith (Israel, J. Gregory, Edward, and Charles). One other last name appears four times in Vermont's list of governors. Which one is it?

Which Vermont governor (of those listed on the right):

_____ 631. had a woman lieutenant governor?

_____ 632. died in office?

_____ 633. was the first to serve two two-year terms?

_____ 634. served the longest?

a. Weeks
b. Johnson
c. Hoff
d. Washburn

635. Which of the following was *not* one of Ethan Allen's brothers?

a. Ira
b. Ebenezer
c. Heman
d. Levi

636. Ethan Allen was captured by the British in the Revolutionary War and spent nearly three years in captivity.

a. True
b. False

637. It was lumber from the forests of Vermont that went into the ships that delayed the British from attacking Fort Ticonderoga in 1776 at the decisive battle of Valcour Island. Historian Earle Newton says of this event, in *The Vermont Story*, "from the virgin forests of Vermont this stubborn, energetic leader had constructed a navy of his own." This leader was

a. Ethan Allen.
b. Ira Allen.
c. Benedict Arnold.
d. Seth Warner.

638. Identify: Hazzen's Line

The New Hampshire colonial governor that "granted" the land for over 125 towns in Vermont was named Benning (639.) _____. The first town he granted was (640.) _____. The intention was to make each town a square of (641.) _____ miles on a side. The charters provided town lots for schools, the Church of England, the first settled minister, and (642.) _____.

639.	640.	641.	642.
a. Allen	a. Norwich	a. one	a. a landfill dump
b. Bailey	b. Bennington	b. six	b. a fort
c. Wentworth	c. Dummerston	c. twenty	c. an industrial park
d. Hubbard	d. Hubbardton	d. thirty	d. himself

643. Identify: Captive Johnson

644. Some of Vermont's most serious historians are members of the Mayflower Society, Vermont Chapter. What is it?

645. Vermont's last legal execution (by the electric chair) took place in what year?

   a. 1938
   b. 1954
   c. 1963

646. He was the most famous scout and Indian fighter of the last and most decisive of the French and Indian Wars. His exploits included the incredible raid on the St. Francis Indians in 1759. He became a true legend on the northern frontier. He is called by Ralph Nading Hill a "bulwark of the frontier." Says Hill, "there has never been a more fearless scout and Indian fighter." His name was?

647. Justin Morgan worked as a _____ in Randolph.

   a. blacksmith
   b. schoolmaster
   c. innkeeper
   d. newspaper editor

Locate These War Memorials Found in Vermont Towns

With the Trinity Catholic Church, Rutland County, town of
(648.) _____.

With the Congregational
Church, Orleans County,
town of
(649.) _____.

With the Town Hall, Addison County, town of (650.) _____.

With the First Congregational Church, Bennington County, town of (651.) _____.

Answers:
Footprints on Granite

561. d. Iroquois. (Vermont was known on ancient maps as "Iroquoisia.")
562. d. not determined by the editors.
563. They were both great lumbermen of the north country. Van Dyke was in truth a New Hampshire man, although he was born in Quebec. But his father was born in Highgate. He rose from nothing and became the "most potent force the whole length of the Connecticut" according to Robert E. Pike, whose *Tall Trees, Tough Men* will prickle the spine of anyone who has spent time in the woods with saw and team and anyone else with enough sense to believe there was a time when guts, endurance, and the capacity to accept pain were a part of everyday life. Van Dyke operated a saw mill at McIndoe Falls and built the Upper Coos Railroad of Vermont. For years he ran his lumber company from Bloomfield, Vermont. When he died at a Connecticut River drive at Turner's Falls in 1902, he was a multimillionaire. Dan Bosse was called by Pike the "greatest riverman in the north country." He left his job with the Brown Paper Company to participate in the last great drive on the Connecticut in 1915, which consisted of five hundred rivermen who floated sixty-five million feet of logs down the river the full length of Vermont's eastern border and beyond.
564. a. Thomas Chittenden.
565. d. Madeleine Kunin.
566. To drive out the Yorkers.
567. c. Jacob Bayley
568. b. False. It was only *three* different states: Vermont, Kentucky, and Arkansas.
569. a. 1867. It is one of the oldest town fairs in the U.S.
570. In the late 1700's it meant hauling a "Yorker" off the ground strapped in a chair, often up to a sign outside an inn.
571. b. Barre.
572. b. Hubbardton.
573. b. Westminster.
574. a. Because Vermont favored abolition of slavery.
575. Gen. John Stark
576. They all served as presidents of railroads. (Paine headed the Vermont Central Railroad; Fairbanks, the Connecticut and Passumpsic Railroad; Smith, the Vermont and Canada Railroad; and Page, the Rutland Railroad.)

577. c. was abolished in 1972. Thereafter, the Department of Social Welfare handled assistance to the poor.
578. a. 1828.
579. Tythingmen were local police.
580. Deerrifts enforced the deer laws.
581. Haywards kept cattle from breaking through fences and impounded stray cattle if necessary.
582. 1848
583. 1888
584. 1958, William Meyer
585. 1816
586. 1881
587. 1954
588. 1905
589. 1791
590. 1962, Phil Hoff
591. 1780 (The man who wrote "Yankee Doodle," a soldier named Giles Gibb, was killed when the Indians raided Royalton.)
592. 1777
593. 1775
594. 1946
595. 1979
596. 1973
597. 1984
598. 1832
599. 1910
600. 1967
601. 1870
602. 1923
603. 1789. He was fifty-four years old.
604. 1800
605. 1867
606. 1890
607. 1931
608. 1933
609. 1970
610. a. Mary Fletcher in Burlington.
611. New Connecticut
612. b. artists.
613. d. Rupert. (Surely you didn't guess Dover, which is in *Windham* County.)
614. b. Freedom and Unity.
615. c. Isle La Motte. Although Fort Dummer in the town of Brattle-

boro was the first *permanent* white settlement in Vermont, the first white settlement was established in 1666 by Captain Pierre La Motte. The French tore it down about ten years later.

616. b. the Haldimand Negotiations.

617. Chittenden had sight in only one eye.

618. the Irasburg Affair

619. Arlington

620. Lt. Gov. S. Hollister Jackson drowned in the flood of 1927.

621. c. The state was losing population.

622. c. Act 250 was in effect.

623. a. The Vermont State Senate was in operation.

624. c. windmill. Baldwin's windmill was to pump water for the village. Robert Hagerman reported in the *Vermont History News* in 1983 that "initial newspaper reports billed it as the tallest in the United States but two weeks later that boast had blossomed to the tallest in the whole world, a claim which Baldwin himself later made in no uncertain terms." Baldwin, however, ran into a consistent problem with windmills in Vermont—not enough wind. Within six months a steam engine had been installed to help out.

625. At the most decisive moment in the most decisive phase of the most decisive battle in the Civil War (the Battle of Gettysburg), Stannard flanked the charging Confederates under General Pickett. The Vermont Historical Society calls it this way in the September 1972 issue of *News and Notes:* "When the Confederate forces began to group for the charge on Cemetery Ridge, they formed two lines that somehow became separated and had to regroup while moving up the slope of Cemetery Ridge in front of the two Vermont brigades. Stannard's bugles sounded as he wheeled his troops to attack the Confederates on their right flank. The surprise was decisive: The Confederates broke in disorder and surrendered by the hundreds."

626. During the nineteenth century a miners' riot occurred at the Ely copper mine in Vershire, Vermont. It was put down by the state militia in what is known as the "Ely War."

627. c. Catamount

628. a. Bennington

629. Seth Hubbell was a well-known Vermont pioneer who settled in Wolcott in 1789. Hubbell's account of the hardships of living in early Vermont should be read by every Vermonter today who thinks life is tough in the Green Mountain State.* We were struck too by the words of Carroll Hubbard of Kirby. Carroll, Seth's great-grandson, was born in Elmore in 1881 and left Vermont about the

*You can find it in Volume II of Abby Hemenway's *Vermont Historical Gazetteer.*

turn of the century. The Vermont Historical Society preserved his words for us in 1976, when he was ninety-four years old.

> Around 1954, just after my dear wife died, passed on after fifty-two years of marriage, I decided to move back to Vermont. I was seventy-five and wanted to go home. I wasn't a young man by any means . . .
>
> This piece of land here was a forest when I began clearing it at the age of eighty-two. The whole area was choked with big logs and brush and stone. I had to clear it just like my great-grandfather cleared the land when he first came up.
>
> I like to travel a lot these days—still drive whenever I want. I often go over to the North Danville area where my father and mother used to live—where we all attended Old North Church.
>
> I'm a Vermonter at heart. All my people have lived up here. I couldn't think of another place I wanted to come home to after being away for so many years.

630. Proctor
631. b. Joseph B. Johnson (Consuelo Bailey, lieutenant governor).
632. d. Peter T. Washburn (1869–1870)
633. a. John E. Weeks (1927–1931)
634. c. Philip H. Hoff (1963–1969)
635. b. Ebenezer. This was the cousin Ethan was drinking with the night before he died.
636. a. True
637. c. Benedict Arnold.
638. Hazzen's Line was the much-disputed border line between Vermont and Massachusetts. The dispute formally began with a proclamation by King George II in 1740 and ended, finally, almost two hundred years later in 1933 with a decision by the Supreme Court of the United States.
639. c. Wentworth
640. b. Bennington
641. b. six
642. d. himself
643. Captive Johnson was the daughter of Mrs. Suzanne Johnson, born on the trail after an Indian raid on Deerfield, Massachusetts. Earle Newton places the town of birth as Cavendish. She spent the first few years of her life in various Indian camps, prisons, the households of the French in Canada, and a boat between North America and England. Her mother, according to Ralph Nading Hill in *Yankee Kingdom*, lived a life of incredible hardship but survived to report:

> My daughter, Captive, still keeps the dress she appeared in when brought to my bedside by the French nurse at the hospital; and often

refreshes my memory with the past scenes, when showing it to her children. . . .

My aged mother, before her death, could say to me, arise daughter and go to thy daughter, for thy daughter's daughter has got a daughter; a command which few mothers can make and be obeyed.

644. It is an association of genealogists. Write Norman Case of Bethel for details.

645. b. In 1954 Donald Demag and Francis Blair were executed in Windsor for killing a Springfield woman during an escape.

646. Robert Rogers. It is difficult for those reared in the ease and comfort of post-war America to truly understand the raw magnitude of the suffering endured and the courage displayed by men like Robert Rogers. Reading Ralph Nading Hill helps, however. One of the editors of this volume was given *The Winooski: Heartway of Vermont* early in life by his Aunt Polly and then later *Yankee Kingdom*. It still brings goose bumps when Hill recalls with us, for instance, Whittier's lines about Robert Rogers:

> Robert Rawlin!—Frosts were falling
> When the Ranger's horn was calling
> Through the woods to Canada . . .

647. a. blacksmith

648. Danby

649. Coventry

650. Goshen. The entirety of downtown Goshen is in the picture—the Town Hall, the Town Office Building, and far in the distance to the left of the Town Office Building, the Town Garage. Now there's a government. (The woman in the picture is a flatlander, born in Brooklyn and raised in New Jersey.)

651. Manchester

THE MADELEINE KUNIN PAGE

Everyone knows that Madeleine Kunin was Vermont's first woman governor. What are her other "firsts"?

	She Was The First	She Was Not the First
652. First woman elected to a state-wide office other than the lieutenant governorship.*	_____	_____
653. First woman defeated by Richard Snelling in the general election for governor.	_____	_____
654. The first governor since World War II born in another country.	_____	_____
655. The first Democratic governor to serve when the Speaker of the Vermont House of Representatives was a Democrat.	_____	_____
656. The first Democratic lieutenant governor ever to serve in Vermont when the governor was a Republican.	_____	_____
657. The first Democratic lieutenant governor in this century to lose a gubernatorial bid in the general election.	_____	_____
658. The first Democratic lieutenant governor in this century ever to be elected governor.	_____	_____
659. The first Burlington resident to be elected governor since World War II.	_____	_____
660. The first Democratic candidate for governor to carry Addison County since Philip Hoff.	_____	_____
661. The first candidate in this century belonging to one of the two major parties to lose a general election for governor in one election and win the governorship in the following election.	_____	_____

*The other state-wide offices are auditor, secretary of state, attorney general, and treasurer.

The answers to this section begin on page 112.

Answers:
The Madeleine Kunin Page

652. No. While Kunin herself was elected lieutenant governor in 1978, and Consuelo N. Bailey was elected lieutenant governor in 1955, in 1974 Stella B. Hackel was elected state treasurer.
653. No. In 1976 Snelling defeated Stella B. Hackel, another Democrat.
654. No. In 1954 Joseph B. Johnson, who was born in Norway, was elected governor as a Republican and served two terms.
655. No. Timothy J. O'Connor, Jr., served as Speaker in 1975–76 when Tom Salmon was governor.
656. Yes.
657. No. John Daley, lieutenant governor under Philip Hoff, lost to Deane Davis in 1968.
658. Yes.
659. No. Philip Hoff, another Democrat, was the first and only other one.
660. No. Tom Salmon did in 1974.
661. Yes. The only other possible candidates for this honor are Percival W. Clement and Dick Snelling. But Clement lost as a Local Option candidate in 1902 and lost as an Independent–Democrat in 1906 before winning as a Republican in 1918. Dick Snelling also won the governorship after losing it to Hoff, but several elections separated his loss from his eventual victory, too.

CHAPTER 12

Believe It or Not

Vermont is such a unique state, it often defies categorization on many aspects of Americana. Because it is so different many have trouble deciphering fact from fiction and myth from reality.

Which of the statements below do you think are believable?

	I Believe It	*I Don't Believe It*
662. The boulders placed strategically along Burlington's Church Street Marketplace for decorative purposes were imported from New Hampshire.	_____	_____
663. Four out of Vermont's last five governors were born outside Vermont.	_____	_____
664. In 1878, seventeen deer were imported from New York State because we'd run out of them in Vermont.	_____	_____
665. The Shelburne Museum is actually located in the town of Charlotte.	_____	_____
666. Burlington, Vermont, is the second cloudiest city in America.	_____	_____
667. Comedian Bob Hope attended the University of Vermont for one year.	_____	_____

The answers to Chapter 12 begin on page 119.

668. Mount Philo in Chittenden County was once an island. _____ _____

669. There are more cows than people in Vermont. _____ _____

670. It is still legal for a Vermont town to go "dry" (forbid the sale of alcoholic beverages), and some still do. _____ _____

671. In 1896 the bones of a great white shark were uncovered in a swamp near Lake Dunmore. _____ _____

672. The cities of Burlington, Rutland, and Brattleboro sponsored programs in 1983 to provide whistles to hang around the necks of their citizens to blow when attacked by criminals. _____ _____

673. In 1848 the bones of a wooly mammoth were uncovered in Mt. Holly, Vermont. _____ _____

674. Congressman James Jeffords is really a Democrat. _____ _____

675. The mountains of the Northeast Kingdom are really New Hampshire's White Mountains. _____ _____

676. There are 3,021 counties in the United States. Vermont has only fourteen of them. Yet nine of the country's twenty-five counties voting most strongly for John Anderson in the presidential election of 1980 were Vermont counties. _____ _____

677. Ethan Allen was not born in the United States. _____ _____

678. Some of the opening scenes of Vermont on the "Bob Newhart Show" were filmed in Maine. _____ _____

679. The Barre Historical Society

Museum is actually located in Montpelier. _____ _____

680. In 1973 the remains of a three-thousand-year-old Indian culture were found during excavations in Swanton. _____ _____

681. As late as 1965, towns like Victory (population 46) and Stratton (population 38) each sent one legislator to the House of Representatives in Montpelier, while towns like Rutland (population 12,000) and Burlington (population 38,000) sent only one also. _____ _____

682. Vermont's last legal execution by hanging took place in Hardwick in 1928. _____ _____

683. When the Green Mountain Boys were formed as a regiment in the Revolutionary War, Ethan Allen was not chosen to lead them. _____ _____

684. In 1849, bones uncovered in a railroad bed excavation near Charlotte were found to be the bones of a whale. _____ _____

685. Montpelier has the smallest population of any capital city of the fifty states. _____ _____

686. In 1968 it cost George Aiken $4.28 to run for reelection to the U.S. Senate. _____ _____

687. Burlington was the first Vermont town or city ever to elect a socialist mayor. _____ _____

688. A wedding rehearsal was taking place on the Bedell Covered Bridge when it was demolished by a hurricane. _____ _____

689. Vermont cast 85% of her vote for Lincoln in 1860.

690. In the presidential election of 1860 the man running against Abraham Lincoln was a native Vermonter.

691. No state lost a greater percentage of its sons in the Civil War than Vermont.

692. Every year the entire state of Vermont defies gravity and rises into the air.

693. The Sheldon Museum is actually located in Middlebury.

694. The American flag, featuring the "stars and stripes," was first used in battle in Vermont.

695. "Moonlight in Vermont" is the Vermont State Song.

696. In the 1984 election, Danny Gore received 2,160 write-in votes for governor.

697. The most expensive college in the nation to attend is located in Vermont.

698. Calvin Coolidge grew up, died, and was buried in Vermont but he did not carry his home town in the presidential election of 1924.

699. Explorer Jacques Cartier was the first white man to look upon the land that became Vermont.

700. The town of Brattleboro was named for Col. William Brattle.

701. The town of Shaftsbury was named for Maj. Given Shaft.

	I Believe It	*I Don't Believe It*

702. The town of Waitsfield was named for Gen. Benjamin Wait. _____ _____

703. The cash value on the sale of Christmas trees in Vermont is more than that on the sale of maple products. _____ _____

704. There was a man on the cover of the first issue of *Vermont Woman* magazine. _____ _____

705. Bow-and-arrow deer hunting is not permitted on Sundays. _____ _____

706. Vermont's black bear population boasts one bear for every three square miles. _____ _____

707. The township of Thetford, population 2,188, has four different functioning post offices. _____ _____

708. More people die every year from all causes in Vermont per capita than in the average American state. _____ _____

709. The first patriot to shoot a British soldier in the Revolutionary War was a Vermonter. _____ _____

710. Vermont has a special season for deer hunters who want to use crossbows instead of guns. _____ _____

711. The Vermont State Flower, the red clover, is not indigenous to Vermont and was imported from England. _____ _____

712. The official Vermont State Nut is the butternut. _____ _____

713. As of 1980 no state had a smaller population than Vermont. _____ _____

714. The *New York Times,* the *New York*

Tribune, and the *New York Daily News* (the nation's largest daily for years) were all founded by Vermonters.   _____   _____

715. Vermont Royster, former editor of the *Wall Street Journal,* was not born in Vermont.   _____   _____

716. A substantial majority of high schools in Vermont still offer Latin.   _____   _____

717. The first president of the University of South Dakota was from Newfane, Vermont.   _____   _____

718. In the nineteeth century, women actually received higher wages as Vermont schoolteachers than did men.   _____   _____

719. Vermont high-school students score higher on SAT's than the national average.   _____   _____

720. Vermont declared war on Germany in September 1941, months before Pearl Harbor and America's entry into the war.   _____   _____

721. Vermont has never executed a woman.   _____   _____

Answers:
Believe It or Not

662. False.
663. True. Madeleine Kunin was born in Switzerland, Dick Snelling in Pennsylvania, Thomas Salmon in Ohio, and Philip Hoff in Massachusetts. Only Deane Davis was a Vermonter.
664. True.
665. If it were, it would be called the Charlotte Museum.
666. True. In Seattle (the cloudiest city in America), the sun shines 50% of the time. In Burlington it shines 51% of the time.
667. False.
668. True.
669. False.
670. True. The towns are Athens, Baltimore, Maidstone, Holland, and Weybridge. Nineteen others have voted "wet" for beer and wine, but "dry" for liquor.
671. You've seen too many movies!
672. False. Only the city of Burlington did this.
673. True.
674. Sometimes he is and sometimes he isn't.
675. True.
676. True. Vermont ranked second overall on the list of states for Anderson.
677. True. Ethan Allen was born in a British colony which was to become the American state of Connecticut.
678. False. The scenes are actually from New Hampshire and Vermont.
679. False. It's located in Barre, of course.
680. True.
681. True.
682. False. Vermont's last hanging took place in 1912 in Windsor.
683. True. Seth Warner was elected instead.
684. True.
685. True.
686. False. It was a much greater amount—$17.09.
687. False. Barre had a socialist mayor in 1912.
688. True. This happened less than two months after a quarter of a million dollars was raised and spent for repair and preservation of the bridge.
689. False. 75%.
690. True.
691. True.

692. Vermont actually "grows" one to two centimeters each year.

693. Of course—any fool knows that!

694. True. In the Battle of Bennington.

695. False. It's "Hail, Vermont," adopted in 1938.

696. False. Vermonters don't waste their votes.

697. True. It cost $16,950 (room, board, and tuition) to attend Bennington College in 1986.

698. False. Silent Cal carried Plymouth 165–7 for 96% of the two-party vote. (The Progressives got one vote.) State-wide he received 83%.

699. False. It was Samuel de Champlain in 1609.

700. True.

701. Nope.

702. True. Benjamin Wait fought with Robert Rogers as a Ranger, was a Green Mountain Boy and one of the prominent early founders of the Vermont Republic. He was Waitsfield's first representative in the state legislature.

703. False, but it's close. In 1984 the cash value of maple products was $10 million while the cash value of Christmas trees was $7 million.

704. True. Among other women pictured, Louvenia Bright was shown with her children and her *husband*.

705. False.

706. True. Vermont has one of the most dense black bear populations in the country.

707. False. It has *six*! They are at Thetford Center, Post Mills, Thetford, East Thetford, West Thetford, and Ely. (Technically, the Ely post office is two hundred feet over the line in Fairlee.)

708. True.

709. True.

710. False. It is illegal to use a crossbow.

711. True.

712. False. Vermont has no state nut.

713. False. Vermont's population was 511,000, but Wyoming and Alaska were lower with 470,000 and 402,000 respectively.

714. You should believe this one. Horace Greeley from Poultney founded the *Tribune*, George Jones, also from Poultney, was co-founder of the *Times*, and William Field of Rutland founded the *Daily News*.

715. Vermont historian Charles Morrissey reported in 1978 that he knew of no Vermonter named "Vermont." The only person he had ever discovered with the first name "Vermont" was Vermont Royster, but he was born and raised in North Carolina. Morrissey, in an article entitled "Names from Vermont History" (*Vermont Life's Annual Guide*, 1978), also reports David Ludlum's discovery of a

beauty of a Vermont name—a minister in Bridport named Increase Graves.

716. True, forty-four schools (73%) offer Latin.

717. False. Webster Merrifield of Newfane was the first president of the University of North Dakota.

718. False. In 1847 men received $12/month and board, while women lived on $4.75. By 1890 men received $38.10 (no board) and women $24.40.

719. True. On the verbal SAT, Vermonters averaged 441 compared to the national average of 431. Vermonters are also higher on math scores, averaging 478 while the national average is 475.

720. False, but we almost did! The legislature passed a resolution that came very close to a declaration of war.

721. False. We hanged two.

722.

Which town had the smallest population according to the 1980 census?

a. Goshen
b. Granby
c. Stratton
d. Victory

Answer

d. Victory had the smallest population with 56 residents. Granby had 70, Stratton had 122, and Goshen had 163.

CHAPTER 13

Vermont ID's

Every student is familiar with the dreaded ID, that simple little term that says, "Do you know anything about me?" Sometimes they are preceded by the command, "*identify* the following," or "*describe* the following," or "*explain* the significance of the following." We simply say: demonstrate that you could engage in a conversation with a real Vermonter when it hinged on an understanding of:

723. A Stanchion

A device designed to hold cattle in their stalls (usually for milking purposes). It is V-shaped with the open end on top. When the cow sticks her head through it, one side is quickly closed toward the other and latched. The cow cannot pull her head back out and thus is held securely in place.

724. Horn of the Moon

A road in Washington County, a cafe in Montpelier, and a pond in East Montpelier. In *Vermont Place-Names*, Esther Swift tells us that "an old Indian is given credit for the picturesque East Montpelier place-name, Horn of the Moon. It seems that once he lost his wife, and later found her at the place he called 'horn of the moon.' A school at the intersection of two country roads has always been called Horn of the Moon school."

725. Monadnock

Charles W. Johnson, in his *Nature of Vermont*, defines one as follows: "Monadnocks are large-scale intrusions of younger rock into pre-existing

The answers to Chapter 13 begin on page 131.

rocks, having squeezed into cracks, pockets, or caverns in a molten state, then solidifying. Most monadnocks are much younger than the host rock into which they have flowed." Mount Ascutney is a monadnock. The more popular meaning is for that of a free-standing or lonely mountain. The Abenaki translation for monadnock is "mountain which sticks up like an island." There is a mountain named Monadnock Mountain in the town of Lemington, Vermont, a solitary and beautiful "monadnock" of 3,140 feet elevation between Willard Stream and Mill Brook. One of the indications of the loneliness of this mountain is that it is omitted from the *Vermont Atlas and Gazetteer*'s list of mountains for hiking even though smaller mountains are included. Perhaps there aren't enough tourists in that part of the kingdom to warrant its mention.

726. German Browns

These are trout brought to Vermont from Europe in the 1800's. They attain much larger sizes than brook trout and can tolerate streams with more silt and warmer water temperatures. There are many good brown trout streams in Vermont. We won't mention our particular favorites, but other equally good ones are the Black River (Ludlow), the Walloomsac (Bennington), and the Missisquoi (Lowell).

727. A "Skipper"

This is a slang expression for a small deer. Often "button-horned bucks" or small does, they are facing their first deer season. Instead of running like adult whitetails, they seem to "skip" along. With the end of the prohibition against shooting antlerless deer, less experienced hunters sometimes shoot these little deer thinking them, in the excitement of the moment, mature does. Often they are left in the woods to spare the hunter the embarrassment of having to tie them on their car and check them in. No matter. They would have starved to death anyway—or so we are told.

728. Spigot

Another term for a sap spout.

729. Draw-off

When a tie occurs in a cattle pull (horses, ponies, or oxen), a "draw-off" is held to determine the winner. (Also used to refer to the process of drawing-off the syrup from a pan of hot sap.)

730. Comforter

Another term for a quilted bed covering.

731. Wagon Tongue

That part of the wagon which protrudes from the front end and to which the pole is attached.

732. Mount Ascutney Train

A pathway of rocks and boulders that originated from Mount Ascutney and were carried from there all the way into Massachusetts by the last glacier. It is said that in the heat of summer in the nineteenth century, one could hear from atop that mountain in Windsor County the distant angry murmur of what one might call the "Mount Ascutney Curse" echo up from the southern terrain as men and women sweated to remove these rocks from their fields. Today as we let these open lands revert to brush or build "condo villages" right smack dab in the middle of them—ignoring the incredible human "sunk costs" that went into their creation—perhaps we should listen again for the bygone wail of the "Mount Ascutney Train."

733. Timberdoodles

Another name for woodcocks. These small game birds are native to Vermont and are often found in alder swales or in woodland pastures near meadows. They like moist ground. Woodcocks migrate down from Canada in the autumn. When startled they often fly straight up like a helicopter. Hunting season for woodcocks is set each year by the United States Fish and Wildlife Service.

734. Auger

A tool with a spiral cutting edge. Vermonters use tools of this variety on their tractors to replace the old-fashioned post-hole diggers that used muscle power. They are also popular these days among ice fishermen. Readers familiar with *The Right Stuff* or Chuck Yeager's popular autobiography will recognize the phrase "auger in." Test pilots came up with a pretty graphic description for a spinning F–104 as it crashed into the ground— especially if you've ever used a hand auger to drill a hole in a beam.

735. Clearcut

When foresters harvest nearly all of the trees in one area. How big must a "clearcut" be to be a real clearcut? Vermont's Fish and Wildlife Department tells us in their publication "Habitat Highlights" that the width must be "at least large enough to remove most of the competitive influence from the uncut area. Usually a minimum of twice the standing tree height." Although often frowned upon, naturalists now tell us that controlled clearcutting can be good for certain wildlife species and timber production.

736. Vermont Yankee

The Vermont Nuclear Power Plant located in Vernon. It went on line in 1972 and has a capacity of 540 megawatts, 219 of which are used by Vermonters. Vermont Yankee provides the state with one-third of its power.

737. Snow Rollers

Nature's snowballs. When a combination of light sticky snow and high winds occurs, the wind actually begins to roll small loops of snow across open fields. As they roll, they gather size and weight. If conditions are right, snow rollers have been reported in sizes up to eighteen inches in diameter.

738. Australian Ballot

A paper ballot (an idea which originated in Australia) listing candidates for election to public office which is distributed inside the polling place and marked secretly by the voter. In Vermont it has come to mean simply election by ballot on town meeting day rather than election *during* (and as part of) the town meeting. If you elect your town officers by "Australian" ballot, the practical meaning is that you don't have to attend town meeting itself to vote for town officers. Some suspect we continue to use the term to confuse newcomers. But of course we don't.

739. Stone Boat

A flat bed of planks (three to four feet wide and six to ten feet long) with very small rails (two to three inches or so) around the outside onto which stones are rolled. The "stone boat" is then drawn over the ground to a rock pile or stone wall site and tipped over (if the farmer has staged his approach wisely) or unloaded. The front of the boat is curved upward so it will slide easily over rough ground. The stone boat is Vermont's most classic symbol of raw, dusty, sweat-soaked, back-breaking, pebbles-in-your-shoes and grit-on-your-tongue labor. The only way to love a stone boat is to pick stone for a day using a wagon.

740. The Common

This is an easy one. It is the village green, the public land usually found in the center of the village. The word originates in a time when the "public weal" was more pronounced and when sense of community was more real. It comes from a time when problems and dreams alike were held more in "common." Other things were often held in common in those days as well—like hogs and cattle that needed common attention. The term "common" is also a handy urban–rural distinguisher. Cities have parks, small towns and villages have "commons"—Boston Common notwithstanding. For us commoners they will always mean the cries of children on swings, the melody of a band concert in the dusk of June, warm lights over cold snow, the blare of the 4th of July or the sleepy drone of a mid-afternoon summertime; but most of all a common bond of togetherness anchored in the soil that calls us homeward. Color it green. Spell it *Vermont.*

741. Ginger Water

Switchel.

742. The Belle of Brattleboro

Captain Andy Bower's cruise boat on the Connecticut River. It's a forty-nine-passenger river boat featuring midnight cruises, dancing, and sunsets.

743. The "Beech Seal"

In early Vermont when disputes over land titles arose, a good whipping with a beech rod was considered by many Vermonters to be a more appropriate means of "conflict resolution" than adherence to the seal on a proclamation by a colonial governor from New York or New Hampshire.

744. The Homer W. Dixon

The only freshwater windjammer cruises in America can be had on her from Perkins Pier in Burlington. She sails on trips up to six days.

745. Switchel

A cooling drink popular on the farms of Vermont in times past. It is made with various combinations of water and ginger and molasses and vinegar. It is often called "ginger water."

746. Quimby's

This is one of Vermont's most famous resort areas. Located deep in the Northeast Kingdom on Big Averill and Forest Lakes, it is featured in Earle Newton's important history, *The Vermont Story,* as follows: "Up in forest-clad Essex County attractive, red-haired Hortense Quimby now runs [this was written in the late 1940's] the hunting lodge established by her father over fifty years ago. An ardent conservationist and one of the state's best businesswomen, she has developed Quimby's into a family resort, with facilities for the care of children, and guides for the adults who find the wilderness around the Averill lakes a paradise for fishing and hunting." Quimby's is a word synonymous in Vermont with the old-style outdoor resort facility so popular in the first half of the century.

747. The Witch of Wall Street

Hetty Green of Bellows Falls was the richest businesswoman in the world. When she died in 1916 she was worth more than $100 million. According to the Vermont Historical Society's January 1971 issue of *News and Notes*, she "became a familiar on the streets of Bellows Falls, Vermont, for the last forty-two years of her life." She married Edward Green of Bellows Falls in 1867. Richard Ketchum of Dorset has written extensively on "The Witch of Wall Street." She was the quintessential penny pincher. The Vermont Historical Society says she was "surely one of the most peculiar figures ever to live in the Green Mountain State."

748. Ernest Johnson

A black folk singer who traveled through Vermont in the 1940's and 1950's singing songs of Negro culture from the South. Mr. Johnson's visits were a welcome event for children of Vermont's rural schools because class was postponed (something that was a rare treat in those days) and Mr. Johnson sang. He charged no fee although the "hat was always passed." He left a generation of Vermont schoolchildren with love, admiration, and joy.

749. Allemande Left

A maneuver in a square dance. The "gentleman" turns to his left and spins with the "lady" waiting there one full turn. As the turn is completed, the lady is sent back to the left and often the gentleman continues right in a "grand right and left." It is more difficult to describe in writing than it is to do, although it is one of those steps that always seems to foul up newcomers to square dancing.

In driving through Vermont, no matter what your purpose or destination, you are bound to see some cows grazing on rolling green pastures or huddled around the barn. How well can you identify some of the different breeds such as Line-back, Jersey, Holstein, Guernsey, Dutch Belted, Ayrshire, Hereford, or Durham? Can you name the four we have pictured on the following pages?

750. _____

751. _____

752. _____

753. _____

Antiques are a favorite Vermont pastime and business. Below are four rocking chairs. Which type is which?

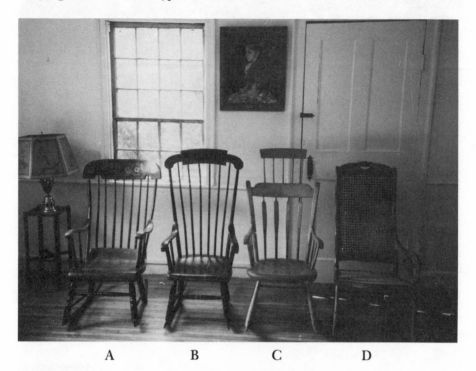

A   B   C   D

_____ 754. Windsor

_____ 755. Boston

_____ 756. Lincoln

_____ 757. Salem

Answers:
Vermont ID's

723.–749. answers appear with the ID
750. Ayrshire
751. Dutch Belted
752. Jersey
753. Holstein
754. c. Windsor
755. a. Boston
756. d. Lincoln
757. b. Salem

758.

The worst train wreck in Vermont history occurred in:

        a. Hartford in 1887.
        b. Essex in 1984.
        c. St. Albans in 1920.
        d. Newbury in 1947.

Answer

a. Hartford in 1887.

Cold temperatures apparently caused a rail to split causing four cars to derail and fall fifty feet onto the ice of the White River from the West Hartford Bridge. Thirty-four died, many from the fires caused by the heat stoves in the wrecked cars on the ice. Forty-nine were injured.

CHAPTER 14

The 14th Original State
Key Numbers for Vermonters

Vermonters, it is well known, like to be precise—mainly when it suits them, as with prices, the depth of snowstorms, and the number of points on their buck. Other times they are not so concerned with precision—as when estimating distances for flatlanders or telling prospective buyers how big the parcel of land really is: "20 acres *more or less.*"

What does each number represent?

759.   70

   a. The road miles (main highway) between Hardwick and Williamstown.
   b. The average IQ of those Vermonters who moved to New Jersey in 1985.
   c. Robert Frost's age at the time of his death.
   d. The population of Granby.

760.   51

   a. The gallons of sap it takes to make a gallon of syrup.
   b. The number of incorporated villages in Vermont.
   c. The mean temperature in Vermont in June.
   d. The number of towns and cities in Rutland and Windham Counties.

761.   150

The answers to Chapter 14 begin on page 136.

a. The number elected to Vermont's House of Representatives.
b. The number of covered bridges in Vermont.
c. The number of times Lt. Gov. Peter Smith uses the word "feel" in a typical 15-minute political address.
d. The average weight of a buck deer shot in Vermont in a typical deer season.

762.   1

a. The number of people Dick Snelling believes are capable of governing Vermont.
b. The number of Democrats Vermonters have elected to represent them in the U.S. Senate since 1850.
c. The number of Vermont mountain peaks above 4,500 feet.
d. The number of U.S. Presidents born in Vermont.

763.   9

a. The number of movies one can choose from on any given night in the Burlington/South Burlington area in 1986.
b. The number of cities in Vermont.
c. The average number of snow days called each year by the Waitsfield elementary school district, 1970–1980.
d. The number of places you can rent home videos in Ludlow.

764.   60

a. Madeleine Kunin's age in 1986.
b. Price of a 1986 hunting license for out-of-staters.
c. Cost of registering a one-ton truck for one year.
d. Number of places you can rent home videos in Milton.

765.   7

a. Maximum number of sap buckets allowed on a maple tree.
b. The most direct route from Middlebury to Brandon.
c. The number of round barns in the state.
d. The number of bars on Burlington's Church Street.

766.   93,135

a. Dollars paid annually to the governor in salary.
b. Tons of salt dumped on Vermont state roads in the winter of 1985–86.
c. People in Chittenden County as of 1980.
d. Registered voters that voted in the last presidential election.

767.   05602

    a. ZIP code for Essex Junction.
    b. ZIP code for Montpelier.
    c. ZIP code for Bennington.
    d. The price of John Deere's most expensive snowmobile.

768.   22

    a. Caliber of Ethan Allen's rifle at Ticonderoga.
    b. Population of Buel's Gore.
    c. Number of Confederates involved in the 1864 St. Albans Raid.
    d. Number of years that George Aiken served in the U.S. Senate.

769.   35

    a. Number of buildings at the Shelburne Museum.
    b. Minimum age required for a gubernatorial candidate.
    c. Number of high schools in the state.
    d. Percentage of Vermont land that is actively farmed.

770.   116

    a. Number of commercial cross-country ski areas in the state.
    b. Number of children's camps operated each summer in Vermont.
    c. Route from Hinesburg to Starksboro.
    d. All of the above.

771.   525,000

    a. Number of cows in Vermont.
    b. Number of registered cars in Vermont, 1986.
    c. Number of wild turkeys in Vermont (not including those found in Montpelier during the legislative session).
    d. Number of gallons of maple syrup produced in 1985.

772.   20

    a. Crossing time in minutes for the Essex Ferry from Charlotte to Essex, New York.
    b. Demerit points causing a month's suspension of your driver's license.
    c. The speed limit on Class II town roads in Vermont.
    d. The number of rainy days in a typical Vermont June.

773.   2

a. The number of towns or cities in Washington County with more than 10,000 inhabitants.
b. The number of teats on a goat.
c. The number of critical national problems Patrick Leahy claims he has solved per week since he was elected to the U.S. Senate in 1974.
d. The number of places Vermont's state capital has been located.

774. 32

a. Length in miles of Lake Memphremagog.
b. Age in years of a maple tree before it produces sap.
c. Miles from Jeffersonville to Stowe when the notch is closed.
d. Average temperature in Vermont in March.

775. 1700

a. Auctions held in the summer of 1985 in Vermont.
b. The year Lake Champlain was discovered.
c. Cost of one semester's tuition to UVM for a Vermont student.
d. Justices of the peace in Vermont in 1985.

776. 15

a. Number of superior judges in Vermont.
b. Cost of a 2-year subscription to *Vermont Life* in 1985.
c. Price of a Vermont "vanity" license plate in 1986.
d. The number of trips the Burlington to Port Kent, New York, ferry takes on an average summer (July 4–August 15) day.

777. 57

a. The price of a one-way PeopleExpress flight from Burlington to Washington, D.C. in 1985.
b. Age of Peter Smith in the year 2000.
c. Golf courses in Vermont.
d. As of May 1985 the number of years that Burlington International Airport has been in operation.

778. 12

a. The legal brook trout limit in Vermont.
b. Number of miles between Brattleboro and Bellows Falls.
c. The number of students that graduated from Vermont's smallest high school in 1986.
d. The price of a ticket to Thunder Road.

Answers:
The 14th Original State

759. d. The population of Granby. (Robert Frost was 89 when he died.)
760. d. The number of towns and cities in Rutland and Windham Counties.
761. a. The number elected to Vermont's House of Representatives. (There are between 114 and 116 covered bridges; sources disagree.)
762. b. The number of Democrats Vermonters have elected to represent them in the U.S. Senate since 1850. (Patrick Leahy.)
763. b. The number of cities in Vermont.
764. b. Price of a 1986 hunting license for out-of-staters.
765. b. The most direct route from Middlebury to Brandon.
766. b. Tons of salt dumped on Vermont state roads. (The governor's salary is in the $60,000 range.)
767. b. ZIP code for Montpelier.
768. c. Number of Confederates involved in the 1864 St. Albans Raid.
769. a. Number of buildings at the Shelburne Museum. (There are 60 public high schools in the state.)
770. c. Route from Hinesburg to Starksboro.
771. d. Number of gallons of maple syrup produced in 1985. (At last count there were 298,119 registered cars and about 200,000 cows, but that was before the brilliant "Buy-Out" program.)
772. a. Crossing time in minutes for the Essex Ferry.
773. b. The number of teats on a goat.
774. a. The length in miles of Lake Memphremagog, although only 5 miles of it are in the U.S. (By the way, it's 26 miles from Jeffersonville to Stowe and the average temperature in March is 28.4 degrees.)
775. d. Justices of the peace in Vermont in 1985.
776. c. Price of a Vermont "vanity" license plate in 1986. (Although *Vermont Life* costs $7.50 a year, you can get a two-year subscription for only $13.95.)
777. c. Golf courses in Vermont. (Smith was born in 1945—you can figure it out.)
778. a. The legal brook trout limit in Vermont.

THE NEW JERSEY PAGE

Probably no other state is compared to Vermont as often as New Jersey. Usually the comparisons are not generated by benign motives; for instance, often you hear "Why don't you go back to New Jersey where you came from!?" or "The minute they get here they try to make the state look just like New Jersey!" As an apology for all the insults cast New Jersey's way over the years, we offer the *New Jersey Page*.

Which State Ranks Higher?

	Vermont	*New Jersey*
779. People per doctor.	_____	_____
780. Public aid recipients as a percentage of population.	_____	_____
781. Unemployment rate.	_____	_____
782. Energy consumption (million BTU's per capita).	_____	_____
783. Infant mortality rate (infant deaths under 1 year old per 1000 live births).	_____	_____
784. Miles of interstate highway.	_____	_____
785. Legal abortions per thousand women 15 years old or older.	_____	_____

The answers to this section begin on page 138.

Answers:
The New Jersey Page

Which state ranks higher?

779. New Jersey
780. New Jersey
781. New Jersey
782. New Jersey
783. New Jersey
784. New Jersey
785. New Jersey

There, we hope this sets the record straight. By the time you finished these 7 questions, you must have realized that we went to great lengths to pick and choose to find data that would show how New Jersey does in fact rank *above* Vermont on many items. We deliberately left out questions on suicide rates, for instance, that showed (as did per capita highway deaths) that New Jersey ranked far *below* Vermont. Who says Vermonters have a bias against New Jersey?

CHAPTER 15

"Not to Me It Don't"
Vermont Punch Lines

To survive among Vermonters, it is imperative to know their humor. As Judson Hale says in his book *Inside New England*, Vermont, like Maine, is a region with a distinctiveness that breeds its own brand of humor. Below we have listed the punch lines of a selection of Vermont jokes. Your task is to supply the story that precedes it. All but two or three are Vermont classics. You should "get" the others too. For more delightful Vermont and New England humor, we suggest Hale's book, which is now out in paperback.

786. "Not to me it don't."

787. "You can't get there from here."

788. "Had a truck like that once myself. Got rid of it."

789. "More'n ten year ago."

790. "and three to talk about how good the old one was."

791. "Compared to what?"

792. "Not yet."

793. "Bury him."

794. "Born here."

795. "Well, I keep my own tom cat."

796. "Always has."

797. "You lose."

The answers to Chapter 15 begin on page 141.

798. "In a balloon."

799. "couldn't have stood another of them Vermont winters."

800. "you can come in and wait."

801. "Nope. I'm still on my horse."

802. "I wouldn't start from here."

803. "Sure it is. But any damn fool knows how to get to Poultney."

804. "I've been against every damn one of them."

805. "Yep, but they'll all be gone in the fall."

Answers:
"Not To Me It Don't"

Jokes

786. Stranger to farmer beside the road: "Does it matter which road I take to Danville?"

787. Tourist to Vermonter: "How is the best way to get to Grafton from here?"

788. A Texan was once bragging to a Vermonter about how huge his ranch was compared to the Vermonter's little hill farm. "Why my ranch is so big," he said, "I can get in my truck on one side of the place, drive all day, and still not reach the other side." The Vermonter paused and said . . .

789. Flatlander to Vermonter: "When did the last train leave for Boston?"

790. How many Vermonters does it take to change a lightbulb? Four. One to screw it in . . .

791. Stranger to old-time Vermonter: "How's your wife?"

792. Newcomer to Vermonter: "This sure is a beautiful town. Lived here all your life?"

793. Out-of-stater to Vermonter: "What are you going to do when old man Pickens dies?"

794. A traveler, having gotten out of his car, wants to cross a very muddy, rut-filled road. He yells out to a Vermonter sitting on the porch of his house on the other side: "Say, how'd you get over there?"

795. Down-stater to Vermonter: "Say, how far is your nearest neighbor?"

796. "Do you suppose it'll ever stop raining?"

797. A talkative lady who was to sit next to President Calvin Coolidge at a dinner party took a wager from a friend that she could not "get three words out of the President all evening." To win the bet she laughingly told Coolidge about the bet at dinner. Solemnly he turned to her and said,

798. A lost balloonist from Ohio who drifts out of the clouds over a small Vermont farm shouts down to a Vermonter in his field, "Where the hell am I?"

799. It is said that once when the Connecticut River rose in the spring it changed course and cut a New Hampshire farmer off, leaving his house and entire farm on the west side of the river in Vermont. But the very next spring the river flooded again and returned to its old channel, shifting the farmer back to the New Hampshire side. "Thank God," he said, "I . . .

141

800. An undertaker was summoned into the hills of Vermont to a farmer's house that was situated a very long way from town. He was to pick up the body of the farmer's wife. Upon his arrival he was met on the porch by the farmer. "She ain't quite dead yet," said he, "but . . .*

801. Once during mud season a man was traveling on a back road and came upon a mudhole in which he found a man buried up to his neck. "You're in trouble, ain't you?"**

802. Summer person to Vermonter beside the road: "Say (they always say "say"), how do you get to Bethel?" Vermonter: "If I were going to Bethel . . .

803. Newcomer to Vermonter: "That Poultney road sign back at the corner is pointing in the wrong direction, isn't it?"***

804. A visitor to the state once encountered an old Vermonter alongside the road. Seeking to strike up a conversation he said, "I bet you've seen a lot of changes in your lifetime." "Yep," came the terse reply. "And . . . ****

805. We like the way Ralph Nading Hill told this one in the Autumn 1950 issue of *Vermont Life*: There was a tourist who "stopped his car on a country road and leaned over the fence to talk with a Vermonter laboring with a hay fork. In the course of the conversation the tourist said, 'You certainly have a lot of characters around here!' Riveting his eyes on the tourist, the Vermonter twanged . . .

*This one, found in Hale's book, was an original for us.

**This story was told by Francis Colburn in his famous speech "A Graduation Address." His wording is of course the funniest. Hear in your imagination the *sound* of a heavy Vermont accent as Colburn, perhaps Vermont's most sought-after public speaker of his time, tells the story: "But, boys and girls, to get back to the parable of the muddy road. That year the mud was so deep on the road that my poor old father had to use snowshoes on the road. As he approached the village he seen a hat lying on that muddy road which, as he came nearer, he observed to be moving. In some consternation, he picked up the hat to find the head of his friend and neighbor, Walter Wheeler.
'Walter,' said my father, 'you're in trouble, ain't you?'
'No,' said Walter, 'for I still have my horse under me.' "

***This is quoted directly from Keith Jennison and Neil Rappaport's *Yup . . . Nope and Other Vermont Dialogues* and is our favorite. Jennison's earlier *Vermont Is Where You Find It* is *the* classic book of Vermont humor. It is because it is also very, very wise.

****Along with several others of these stories, this one can be found in Allen R. Foley's *What the Old-Timer Said* (Brattleboro, Vermont: The Stephen Greene Press, 1971). It's an awfully funny book.

806.

An item sold at an auction in 1974 for $123,000 was the most expensive of its kind in American history. It was only one of eleven known to exist. It was sold by a Dorset man, W.E. Stockhausen. Yet after the sale, another of the eleven left in the world (and the only one in private hands) was *still* owned by a resident of Dorset, Vermont, H. Bradley Martin. What are these most valuable objects?

a. Cows
b. Copies of Edgar Allen Poe's *Tamerlane*
c. First editions of the Vermont commemorative stamp
d. Statuettes carved from Danby marble

Answer

b. Copies of Edgar Allen Poe's *Tamerlane*

CHAPTER 16

Natural Vermont

When Sam Hand and Nick Muller decided to publish an edition of articles on Vermont history, they entitled it *In a State Of Nature*. Good choice. For when one hears the word Vermont, one thinks "natural": one thinks hillsides and ponds and bogs and pastures and forests. And one thinks of the living creatures that crawl, slither, fly, swim, run, flutter, flit, and float above and below, in and among, and roundabout this incredibly beautiful state of ours. Living in Vermont unconscious of the natural world would be like living in Washington unconscious of politics. Or living in Arizona unconscious of the sun. This section judges your capacity to accept Vermont's greatest gift, the chance to live with nature.

807. When do luna moths appear in Vermont? Early June or early August?

808. Although Vermont doesn't have many every year, sultry summer nights do occur from time to time. One of the fascinations of these evenings is the constant flash of fireflies from the deep grasses of meadow and pasture. Why *do* glowworms glow?

809. Between 1959 and 1967 Vermont imported 124 _____ from Maine to help reduce the damage caused by porcupines.

   a. fisher cats
   b. weasels
   c. bobcats
   d. coyotes

The answers to Chapter 16 begin on page 153.

810. One of the earliest memories of the natural world most Vermonters have is watching robins pull worms from the ground to feed their young. How much does a nestling robin eat in a day?

a. 5-7 worms.
b. About 60 inches of worms.
c. About 5 feet of worms.
d. About 14 feet of worms.

811. A porcupine is covered with

a. 100–200 quills.
b. 2,000–3,000 quills.
c. 30,000–40,000 quills.

Vermont is a tough land. We take our pleasures where we find them. One of those pleasures is the birds that sing and swoop or sometimes just sit there and look, well, pretty. Or interesting. Or awesome. See if you can match the bird with the peculiar characteristic attributed to it.

a. Eastern Phoebe
b. Cowbird
c. House Wren
d. Killdeer

_____ 812. Leaves its eggs in other birds' nests and lets them do the upbringing.

_____ 813. Sometimes punctures an opponent's eggs with its bill.

_____ 814. Builds its nest on the ground, not in a tree.

_____ 815. Sees an insect fly by, darts out, catches it, and twitches its tail when perched.

816. You can get arrested these days for being too interested in exotic *grass* found in out-of-the-way places in Vermont. Of the following, which is a real wild grass found in Vermont?

a. Mohawk Grass
b. Barnyard Grass
c. Maple Grass
d. Goldenrod

817. A male white-tailed deer sheds its antlers every winter and grows new ones during the summer.

a. True
b. False

818. Which of the following is *not* a superstition about birds that are found in Vermont?

    a. Barn swallows roosting in your barn will protect it from lightning.
    b. A robin dying in your yard brings bad luck.
    c. Eating mockingbird eggs will cure stuttering.
    d. It is lucky to be defecated on by sea gulls.

819. One of the most frightening sounds one can hear in the woods of Vermont is the howl of a bobcat. In which month are you most likely to hear it?

    a. June
    b. September
    c. January
    d. March

820. Of the following, which is the "Mr. T." of Vermont's summer birds?

    a. The robin
    b. The grackle
    c. The kingbird
    d. The hermit thrush

821. Who wrote the book *Pioneering with Wildflowers*?

For anyone to live happily in Vermont it is essential to know the language—especially those items of the natural world known by popular terms. Here is a list of names you may hear in Vermont. What do they stand for? Some answers may be used more than once.

Answers

_____ 822.	Shepherd's Purse	a. A bird
_____ 823.	Woolly Bear	b. A wildflower
_____ 824.	Stinking Benjamin	c. A caterpillar
_____ 825.	Pine Siskin	d. A turtle
_____ 826.	Bobolink	e. A frog
_____ 827.	Kingfisher	f. A fish
_____ 828.	Stinkpot	g. A duck
_____ 829.	Dutchman's Breeches	h. A butterfly
_____ 830.	Peeper	i. A fern
_____ 831.	"Square Tail"	
_____ 832.	Pumpkin Seed	
_____ 833.	Teal	

_____ 834. "Bog Bull"

_____ 835. "Whistler"

_____ 836. Mourning Cloak

_____ 837. Coltsfoot

_____ 838. Maidenhair Spleenwort

_____ 839. Bullhead

_____ 840. Whippoorwill

841. Wildflowers are a sure sign of spring and, like the coming of the songbirds, are the object of such happy cries as "Guess what I saw today!" One of the following is a rare and beautiful wildflower of Vermont which blooms closer to autumn than spring and like the shortening twilight signals the coming of winter.

   a. The lady slipper
   b. The trailing arbutus
   c. The fringed gentian
   d. The hepatica

842. Which one usually attains a greater weight at maturity, a snapping turtle or a river otter?

843. In the summer you may hear a Vermonter use the term "frond," which is

   a. a frog pond.
   b. Abenaki for "fish."
   c. the leaf of a fern.
   d. one of the implements for making dandelion wine.

844. Vermont is less forested now than it was 100 years ago.

   a. True
   b. False

845. Some ground-nesting birds peep to each other while they are still inside their shells in order to synchronize their hatching.

   a. True
   b. False

846. Vermont has its share of summer thunderstorms. The number of miles you are from the thunderstorm is equal to the number of seconds that elapse between the lightning and the crash of thunder.

   a. True
   b. False

847. One gender of the mallard duck does not quack. Is it the male or the female?

848. Muskellunge, often called "muskie," are not found in Vermont.

   a. True
   b. False

849. There are no documented fatalities from snakebite in Vermont.

   a. True
   b. False

850. One of Vermont's most important naturalists began his public career with a magazine article on the subject of fox hunting in New England. He also published sketches for *Forest and Stream* which reappeared in his book *Uncle Lisha's Shop*. He did most of his writing while blind. He was from Ferrisburg and died in 1900. His name was Rowland Evans _____.

851. Vermont has no poisonous rattlesnakes.

   a. True
   b. False

852. A well-known scene in the Northeast Kingdom in the springtime is a crowd of people gathered near the village of Orleans along the Willoughby River just outside of town. What are they doing?

   a. Observing the fish.
   b. Waiting for the return of native wood ducks.
   c. Watching the "Spring Folly" swimmers.
   d. Watching for migrating snow geese.

853. In Vermont "Thurman Dix," "Turtle," and "Spectacle" are the names of

   a. spring wildflowers.
   b. mushrooms.
   c. birds.
   d. lakes.

854. What is the only fir tree that changes color and loses its needles in the fall?

855. What do you call colonies of nesting great blue herons?

856. The top twig of a hemlock tree always points

    a. east.
    b. west.
    c. north.
    d. south.

857. Dragonflies whiz by you on a summer evening at speeds up to

    a. 20 miles per hour.
    b. 40 miles per hour.
    c. 60 miles per hour.
    d. 80 miles per hour.

Match the wildflower with its other name:

_____	858. Bluets	a. Bells of Peace
_____	859. Rose Pogonia	b. Cowslip
_____	860. Marsh Marigold	c. Cankerroot
_____	861. Goldthread	d. Quaker Ladies
_____	862. American Columbine	e. Snake Mouth

863. Name the wildflower that is also called dragonroot, starch plant, and memory root. Hints: Think church. The roots are edible if cooked or dried out.

864. What do these names have in common?

Peacham
Molly
Franklin
Chickering

865. When was the following quote written?
"The beaver, though formerly a very common animal in Vermont, is probably now nearly or quite exterminated, none of them having been killed within the state, to my knowledge, for several years."

    a. 1853
    b. 1910
    c. 1938
    d. 1974

866. Vermont's world-renowned conservationist of a century ago was George Perkins _____.

867. Perhaps Vermont's most popular nature writer, author of *Loon in*

My Bathtub, How Do You Spank a Porcupine?, *Possum in the Parking Lot*, and other books is _____.

Anyone living in Vermont for the last thirty years or so is aware of the balance between change and permanence. Some things seem to endure forever. Others seem to melt away, slowly and unnoticed. Some things we try to protect. Others we do not.

Below is a list of things found in Vermont. Place them in the proper category of "endangerment."

	These are on the Official Vermont Endangered Species List	These are not on the Official Vermont Endangered Species List	These are not on the Official Vermont Endangered Species List but should be
868. Dutch Elm	_____	_____	_____
869. Indiana Bat	_____	_____	_____
870. Barn Swallow	_____	_____	_____
871. Lake Sturgeon	_____	_____	_____
872. Fisher Cat	_____	_____	_____
873. American Moose	_____	_____	_____
874. Lady Slipper	_____	_____	_____
875. Common Loon	_____	_____	_____
876. Town Meeting	_____	_____	_____
877. Timber Rattlesnake	_____	_____	_____
878. Bearberry Willow	_____	_____	_____
879. Raven	_____	_____	_____
880. Skidway Header	_____	_____	_____
881. Coydog	_____	_____	_____
882. Cowberry	_____	_____	_____
883. Three-Toothed Cinquefoil	_____	_____	_____
884. Real Vermonter	_____	_____	_____

The best way to get accurate information on animal species is to use the animal's Latin name. Can you match them up?

_____	885. Black Bear	a. Castor canadensis canadensis
_____	886. Eastern Bobcat	b. Vulpes vulpes
_____	887. Beaver	c. Ursus americanus
_____	888. White-tailed Deer	d. Marmota monax
_____	889. Red Fox	e. Lynx rufus rufus
_____	890. Woodchuck	f. Odocoileus virginianus virginianus

Two Lakes in the Kingdom

One by a city . . .

It is (891.) _____.

One by itself . . .

It is (892.) _____.

Answers:
Natural Vermont

807. Early June
808. Glowworms glow to attract a mate.
809. a. fisher cats
810. d. 14 feet of worms.
811. c. 30,000–40,000 quills which may come out if touched, but a porcupine cannot "throw" them at an enemy.
812. b. Cowbird
813. c. House Wren
814. d. Killdeer
815. a. Eastern Phoebe
816. b. Barnyard Grass
817. a. True
818. b. A robin dying in the yard. We made that one up. The others are verified in the Fall 1984 Newsletter of the Vermont Institute of Natural Science (VINS). Those that answered "d" because sea gulls are not a Vermont bird have never tried to eat a hamburger outside at any of the fast-food restaurants near Burlington where it is possible to get very lucky very quickly.
819. d. March is their mating season.
820. c. The kingbird. Chris Fitchtel of the Vermont Institute of Natural Science reports driving all the way from Woodstock to go to the rescue of a Rutland family which was being swooped on by nesting kingbirds. Chris succeeded in saving the kingbirds from the homeowner.
821. It was written by George Aiken in 1935.
822. b. Shepherd's Purse is a spring wildflower.
823. c. Woolly Bear is a caterpillar.
824. b. Stinking Benjamin is a wildflower.
825. a. Pine Siskin is a bird.
826. a. Bobolink is a blackbird.
827. a. Kingfisher is a bird.
828. d. Stinkpot is a turtle.
829. b. Dutchman's Breeches is a wildflower.
830. e. Peeper is a tiny frog.
831. f. "Square Tail" is a trout.
832. f. Pumpkin Seed is a fish.
833. g. Teal is a duck.
834. a. "Bog Bull" is an American bittern.
835. g. "Whistler" is the goldeneye duck.

836. h. Mourning Cloak is a butterfly.
837. b. Coltsfoot is a wildflower.
838. i. Maidenhair Spleenwort is a common fern.
839. f. Bullhead is a fish.
840. a. Whippoorwill is a bird.
841. c. The fringed gentian. Richard Headstrom in the Fall 1984 issue of the VINS Newsletter reminded us of William Cullen Bryant's "To the Fringed Gentian":
    "Thou waitest late and com'st alone,
    When woods are bare and birds have flown,
    And frosts and shortening days portend
    The aged year is near its end."
842. A snapping turtle can grow to 3 feet long and weigh 50 pounds while a river otter is usually 25 pounds.
843. c. The leaf of a fern.
844. b. False
845. a. True
846. b. False. After counting the seconds between the lightning and the thunder, you must then divide by five since sound travels a mile in 5 seconds.
847. The male mallard doesn't quack.
848. b. False. The record muskie was 29 pounds 8 ounces caught in 1978.
849. a. True
850. Robinson
851. b. False (there are timber rattlesnakes, especially in southwestern Vermont).
852. a. Watching steelhead rainbows (trout) struggle up the falls near town. They have spent the year in Lake Memphremagog and are migrating to spawn.
853. d. lakes.
854. Tamarack, also called the larch.
855. Rookeries
856. c. north.
857. c. Dragonflies have been timed at 60 miles per hour.
858. d. Quaker Ladies
859. e. Snake Mouth
860. b. Cowslip
861. c. Cankerroot
862. a. Bells of Peace
863. Jack-in-the-pulpit
864. They are all the names of Vermont bogs.
865. a. 1853 in Zadock Thompson's *Natural History of Vermont*.

866. Marsh
867. Ronald Rood

On the List

869. Indiana Bat
871. Lake Sturgeon
874. Lady Slipper
875. Common Loon
877. Timber Rattlesnake
882. Cowberry
883. Three-Toothed Cinquefoil

Not on the List

868. Dutch Elm*
872. Fisher Cat
873. American Moose
878. Bearberry Willow
879. Raven
881. Coydog

Should be on the List

870. Barn Swallow**
876. Town Meeting***
880. Skidway Header****
884. Real Vermonter

885. c. Black Bear—Ursus americanus
886. e. Eastern Bobcat—Lynx rufus rufus
887. a. Beaver—Castor canadensis canadensis

*Even though they are fast disappearing in Vermont, the splitting maul handle and gasoline-driven wood splitters lobbyists are working hard to keep them off the endangered species list.

**The barn swallow lives in barns, good old-fashioned barns with haylofts and timbers and dark dusty corners. We seem to be losing these.

***We became truly pessimistic about the future of town meeting when a Vermont state senator described in detail and with some fascination a "strange" electoral device he had "discovered" in a town meeting he'd visited recently in one of the smaller towns in his district. It turned out to be the *normal* method of electing officers by ballot during the meeting when a majority is needed to win. When we elect state senators no more familiar with town meeting than that, we'd best get it on the official endangered species list ASAP.

****You don't roll logs on trucks via a "skidway header" any more. You place them on the truck with a huge device perched on the cab called a (log, wood, apple, cherry) picker. (Answer: cherry.)

888. f. White-tailed Deer—Odocoileus virginianus virginianus
889. b. Red Fox—Vulpes vulpes
890. d. Woodchuck—Marmota monax
891. Lake Memphremagog
892. Lake Willoughby

893.

Thaddeus Stevens, the great abolitionist in the United States Congress, was a Vermonter born in Danville. But he was expelled from UVM and finished his college days at Dartmouth. What was his crime?

    a. A panty raid
    b. Ax-murdering a cow
    c. Profanity
    d. Short-sheeting the dean's bed

Answer

  b. Thaddeus Stevens's crime was ax-murdering a cow.

CHAPTER 17

A "Modest Anarchism"
Vermont Politics

If there is one thing for which Vermont is known nationally, it is its politics. Trouble is, most of what is known is wrong! We are known as conservative and Republican. We are neither. True, we were Republican to the very core until the early 1950's. But that has been different for thirty years. We have never been conservative. Poor, perhaps, but never conservative. Vermont has also been known for clean politics. Cynics say that's because there isn't any loose loot laying around. Let them talk. We know it's more than that. In *Inside New England*, Judson Hale puts it this way: "It has been said that James Curley of Boston 'could no more have been governor of Vermont than Joe E. Brown could have been the Shah of Iran.' And though Vermont voted for Warren Harding for president in 1920, Harding would have had about as much success as a Vermont politician as, in the words of writer Leonard Morrison, 'a peanut shucker at a corn husk.' " Right on.

Recently Walter Shapiro, a senior editor at *Newsweek*, said in the *New England Monthly* that Vermont was "arguably the most liberal state in the nation." People who insist on using the word "most" to modify words like "liberal" or "conservative" to modify "Vermont" display a fundamental ignorance of the state. We like the words of Paul Goodman, who described our politics as "a modest anarchism and plenty of decentralization," or Bill Schubart, who, lamenting the loss of the native Vermonter to author Annie Proulx of Vershire, called our ways "a fascinating mix of superficially Republican but innately humanistic and radical politics."

The answers to Chapter 17 begin on page 168.

894. Vermont's first primary election was held in which year?

 a. 1870
 b. 1916
 c. 1932
 d. 1952

895. 1902 was a critical year in Vermont politics. In that year

 a. the legislature voted to extend the term of governor from 1 year to 2.
 b. the House of Representatives was reduced in size from 286 members to 246.
 c. a state-wide referendum to allow localities to sell alcoholic beverages was passed.
 d. the "Bull Moose Progressives" elected their candidate governor of Vermont.

896. In the 1950's and the 1960's the Democratic Party made great gains in Vermont. Which of the following candidates received the most votes?

 a. Robert Larrow in a race for governor in 1952.
 b. Frederick Fayette in a race for the senate in 1958.
 c. Russell Niquette in a race for governor in 1960.
 d. Philip Hoff in a race for governor in 1962.

897. In the Vermont primary of 1982 the dimensions of the ballot were

 a. 6 inches by 12 inches.
 b. 10 inches by 11 inches.
 c. 11 inches by 19 inches.
 d. 19 inches by 25 inches.

898. Vermont passed its first law relating to campaign finances in the year

 a. 1816.
 b. 1902.
 c. 1952.
 d. 1972.

Jim Mullin ran for state-wide office once in Vermont. In the (899.)
_____ (party) primary election of (900.) _____ (year), he ran
for (901.) _____ (office).

158

902. How much did it cost Jim for each vote he received?

    a. $.82
    b. $2.78
    c. $20.42
    d. $78.10

903. Which of the following politicians has lost the most state-wide races in Vermont?

    a. Stewart Ledbetter
    b. Peter Diamondstone
    c. Anthony Doria
    d. Dennis Morrisseau

904. If no candidate in the general election for governor receives a majority of the popular vote, then

    a. the candidate with the most votes is declared elected.
    b. a runoff election is held in 6 weeks time between the 2 leading candidates.
    c. a joint assembly of the Vermont House and Senate decide the matter by a plurality vote.
    d. the Vermont Senate decides the matter by a plurality vote.

905. Vermont's primary election is held

    a. the first Tuesday in June.
    b. the second Tuesday in June.
    c. the first Tuesday in September.
    d. the second Tuesday in September.

906. Which of the following offices in Vermont has never been held by a woman?

    a. Auditor of accounts
    b. Treasurer
    c. Lieutenant governor
    d. Secretary of state

907. No one has ever been convicted of a campaign finance law violation in Vermont.

    a. True
    b. False

908. Which of the following political parties that appeared on the Vermont ballot in the last quarter century received the most votes in a state-wide election?

    a. Liberty Union
    b. Citizens Party
    c. Small is Beautiful
    d. Libertarian

909. The widest percentage point gap between the two major party candidates for president occurred in which election? ·

    a. Mondale vs. Reagan in 1984
    b. McGovern vs. Nixon in 1972
    c. Johnson vs. Goldwater in 1964
    d. Kennedy vs. Nixon in 1960

910. The most Democratic municipality in Vermont in the 1984 Presidential election was

    a. Winooski.
    b. Strafford.
    c. Burlington.
    d. Marlboro.

911. There were 49 municipalities reporting votes from the Northeast Kingdom in 1984. How many did Mondale/Ferraro carry?

    a. 0
    b. 5
    c. 15
    d. 35

Name That County
(Choose a county only once)

_____ 912. Strongest for Reagan, 1984.

_____ 913. Strongest for Mondale, 1984.

_____ 914. Strongest for Jeffords, 1984.

_____ 915. Second strongest for Kunin, 1984.

_____ 916. Second strongest for Easton, 1984.

_____ 917. Kunin's best in 1982.

_____ 918. Snelling's best in 1982.

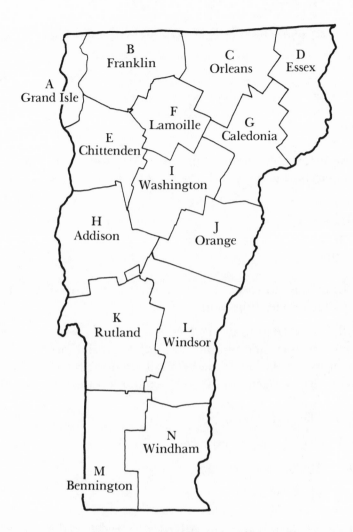

_____ 919. Leahy's best county in 1980 was Chittenden where he got 54.8%. What was his second best county at 54.4%?

_____ 920. Kunin made her largest percentage point gain in Chittenden County in 1984, followed closely by her gain in which county?

_____ 921. The largest percentage for Independent candidate John Anderson came in this county in 1980.

_____ 922. In 1984 Kunin received 48% of the vote in Grand Isle County. Which county most nearly matched that percentage?

_____ 923. In the 1984 presidential race, Lamoille County voted 62.1% for Reagan. Which county was closest on the higher side at 63.5%?

924. How many of Vermont's 246 towns and cities did Mondale carry in 1984?

    a. 0
    b. 18
    c. 61
    d. 96

925. The most Republican municipality in Vermont in the 1984 Presidential election was

    a. Proctor.
    b. Middlesex.
    c. Vernon.
    d. Granby.

Rank the following races according to how close the percentage point gap was between the two leading candidates.

    a. Jeffords vs. Dietz in the 1978 congressional race.
    b. Kennedy vs. Salmon in the 1974 gubernatorial race.
    c. Snelling vs. Hackel in the 1976 gubernatorial race.
    d. Ledbetter vs. Leahy in the 1980 senatorial race.

_____ 926. The closest race.

_____ 927. The second-closest race.

_____ 928. The third-closest race.

_____ 929. The fourth-closest race.

930. Who was the last incumbent governor to be defeated in a general election for reelection?

931. Who was the only incumbent Republican governor ever to lose a primary for reelection to the governorship?

Match the opponents:

Winners	Losers
_____ 932. Snelling (governor, 1978)	a. Snelling
_____ 933. Hoff (governor, 1966)	b. Pollina
_____ 934. Jeffords (U.S. House, 1984)	c. Granai
_____ 935. Aiken (U.S. Senate, 1956)	d. O'Shea

162

Match the office with the candidate that sought it:

_____ 936. governor
_____ 937. U.S. House of Representatives
_____ 938. U.S. Senate
_____ 939. lieutenant governor
_____ 940. attorney general
_____ 941. secretary of state

a. Margaret "Peg"
   Garland
b. Daniel Woodward
c. James Douglas
d. Bruce Lawlor
e. Mark Kaplan
f. Scott Skinner

942. No Democratic candidate for governor other than Philip Hoff has ever carried a majority of Vermont's counties.

a. True
b. False

943. Walter Kennedy, Republican candidate for governor in 1974, was nicknamed _____.

Unlike the president and vice president, Vermont governors and lieutenant governors serving "together" can be members of different parties. Match the lieutenant governor with the governor of the opposite party they served with:

Governor	Lieutenant Governor
_____ 944. Philip Hoff (Democrat)	a. John Burgess (Republican)
_____ 945. Tom Salmon (Democrat)	b. Peter Smith (Republican)
_____ 946. Dick Snelling (Republican)	c. Ralph Foote (Republican)
_____ 947. Madeleine Kunin (Democrat)	d. Madeleine Kunin (Democrat)

948. In Vermont we have a "long" state-wide ballot, electing 6 different officers every 2 years. Have the Democrats ever won all 6 offices at once?

a. Yes
b. No

Although political polls are common these days in Vermont, this was not always the case. Vermont's most famous pollster in the 1960's and early 1970's was Vincent (949). _____ of (950.) _____ College who discovered a "bellwether" town in Vermont named (951.) _____.

163

952. The states are awarded representatives to Congress on the basis of their population. Vermont now sends one. But there was a time when Vermont's population was a larger proportion of the national population and we sent _____ to Washington.

    a. 3
    b. 6
    c. 9

953. It is well known that in 1936, Vermont was one of two states to vote against Roosevelt and for Alfred M. Landon (81,023 to 62,124. The Communist candidate, Earl Browder, got 405 votes). There was one other presidential election in this century in which Vermont was one of two states to vote for a loser. Which one was it?

954. There have been 2 "walkers" for election in recent Vermont history. One was Stewart Ledbetter. The other was

    a. Jim Jeffords.
    b. Randy Majors.
    c. Nathaniel Frothingham.
    d. Pat Leahy.

Match the party with the politician:

_____ 955. Martha Abbott	a. Libertarian
_____ 956. Robin Lloyd	b. Liberty Union
_____ 957. James Hedbor	c. Small is Beautiful
_____ 958. Morris Earle	d. Citizens Party

Match the opponents in the Vermont primary:

Winners	*Losers*
_____ 959. Peter Smith (for lieutenant governor, 1982)	a. Elwyn Kernstock
	b. William G. Craig
_____ 960. Marie Dietz (for U.S. Congress, 1978)	c. Chester Scott
	d. Tom Evslin
_____ 961. Stewart Ledbetter (for U.S. Senate, 1980)	e. Jim Jeffords
_____ 962. Richard Snelling (for governor, 1976)	
_____ 963. Fred Hackett (for governor, 1972)	

964. In the summer of 1986, a political survey reported that _____ of a

random sample of 504 Vermonters could name Sen. Robert Stafford and Sen. Patrick Leahy.

a. 27%
b. 52%
c. 73%

965. How many electoral votes does Vermont have?

966. In 1958 he pulled off a remarkable upset in Vermont politics. He was the first Democrat to be elected to the U.S. House of Representatives from Vermont in this century. Who was he?

967. If you added up all the tax money raised in Vermont to be spent on our state and local highways, the state provided a higher percentage of the total for the years 1942 and 1957 than it did for the years 1982, 1983, and 1984.

a. True
b. False

968. In relation to Vermont's total personal income, the state spent more on total general expenditures in 1983 and 1984 than it did in the years 1976 and 1978.

a. True
b. False

969. Who ran against John Easton for the right to lose to Madeleine Kunin in 1984?

970. He (the answer to question 969) spent about

a. a hundred grand.
b. a quarter of a million.

Match the percentage of the vote received with the Democratic presidential primary candidates in 1984:

_____ 971. Gary Hart   a. 70%
_____ 972. Walter Mondale   b. 20%
_____ 973. Jesse Jackson   c. 8%

974. In 1942 the state's percentage of total state and local expenditures

for public welfare (excluding federal funds) was 56%. In 1984 it was

a. 30%.
b. 60%.
c. 75%.
d. 100%.

975. In 1957 there were 268 full-time employees of state and local
government in Vermont for every 10,000 men, women, and children
in the state. In 1978 there were nearly twice as many, 485. In 1984
there were

a. 464.
b. 498.
c. 540.
d. 630.

976. In 1984 Vermonters paid out $1,183,600,000 in federal taxes. No
state paid less.

a. True
b. False

The pie charts below were developed by Vermont state government for
1987. Fill them in:

Where the Money Comes from

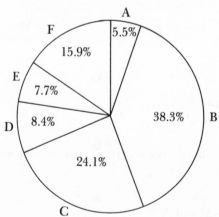

_____ 977. Other Taxes
_____ 978. Meals and Rooms Taxes
_____ 979. Income Taxes

_____ 980. Other Revenues
_____ 981. Corporate Taxes
_____ 982. Sales Taxes

166

Recommendation as to Where It Should Go

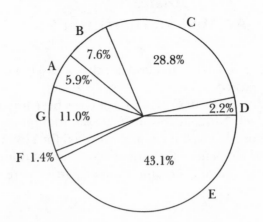

_____ 983. Development

_____ 984. Education

_____ 985. Miscellaneous

_____ 986. General

_____ 987. Human Services

_____ 988. Environment

_____ 989. Protection

Answers:
A "Modest Anarchism"

894. b. 1916
895. c. a state-wide referendum to allow localities to sell alcoholic beverages was passed.
896. c. Philip Hoff won in 1962 with 61,383 votes over Ray Keyser's 60,035. Russell Niquette lost in 1960 even though about 10,000 more Vermonters voted for him than voted for Hoff in 1962.
897. d. 19 inches by 25 inches—the largest state-wide ballot in Vermont's history, mainly because 4 major parties were represented.
898. b. 1902.
899. Republican
900. 1980
901. U.S. Senate
902. d. $78.10. He lost. He spent $957,194 and received 12,256 votes. The first candidate ever to report campaign expenditures in Vermont (he did so voluntarily) was Marshall J. Hapgood, who ran for governor in 1910. He reported $103.76.
903. b. Peter Diamondstone
904. c. A joint assembly decides. The last time it happened in the gubernatorial race was 1853.
905. d. The second Tuesday in September.
906. a. Stella Hackel was elected treasurer in 1974. Madelyn Davidson was appointed treasurer in 1968 and Helen Burbank was appointed secretary of state in 1947.
907. a. True
908. b. The Citizens Party candidate got 25,280 votes (13%) against Jim Jeffords in 1980. Jeffords had no Democratic opposition that year.
909. c. Vermont surprised the nation by giving Goldwater only 34%, well below Goldwater's average state vote.
910. d. Marlboro with 69% for Mondale/Ferraro. The other strong Mondale area was a cluster of towns in the Connecticut River Valley, Norwich (62%), Strafford (63%), and Vershire (50%). Burlington's percentage was 55; Winooski's was 50.
911. a. 0. The Democrats came closest in Brunswick where they tied 21 to 21. If one town voter who cast his or her vote for Sonia Johnson (Citizens Party) had voted Democratic, the town would have become the only one for Mondale/Ferraro. Who says your vote doesn't count?
912. d. Essex County at 69.5%, followed by Caledonia with 68.3%.
913. e. Chittenden County, but only by the teeniest of whiskers. Chit-

tenden County voted 44.44% for Mondale; Washington voted 44.35% for Mondale.

914. k. Rutland County, his home county, gave him 72.9% of the vote.
915. i. Washington County at 53.7%. But once again Chittenden County and Washington County were very close. Chittenden cast 53.8% of its votes for Kunin. All in all the Kunin and Mondale votes for both counties were very closely related in 1984. Unfortunately for Mondale, the relationship always showed him trailing Kunin by a fairly predictable margin.
916. g. Caledonia County with 55.6%. Strongest for Easton was Essex with 56.2%.
917. b. Franklin County with 49.6%. Snelling carried all 14 counties in 1982.
918. j. Orange County with 60% of the vote.
919. a. Grand Isle.
920. l. Windsor County. Her greatest gain—8.7%—came on her home ground, Chittenden County. Windsor's percentage increase was 8.6%. All in all Kunin drew 17,761 more votes from these two counties in 1984 than she did in 1982.
921. n. Windham County, where he received 19.1% of the vote.
922. m. Bennington County at the other end of the state. So much for regional politics.
923. c. Orleans County. Maybe there is a regional vote in Vermont after all.
924. b. 18
925. d. Granby voted 42 to 6 (87.5%) for Reagan/Bush. Right behind was Maidstone at 41 to 6. The other percentages are Proctor (58%), Middlesex (47%), and Vernon (76%).
926. d. Ledbetter vs. Leahy. (Leahy won by 1%.)
927. c. Snelling vs. Hackel. (Snelling won by 13%.)
928. b. Kennedy vs. Salmon. (Salmon won by 19%.)
929. a. Jeffords vs. Dietz. (Jeffords won by 54%.)
930. F. Ray Keyser, Jr. Philip Hoff beat him in 1962.
931. Mortimer Proctor in 1946.
932. c. Snelling vs. Granai
933. a. Hoff vs. Snelling
934. b. Jeffords vs. Pollina
935. d. Aiken vs. O'Shea
936. b. governor—Daniel Woodward
937. e. U.S. House—Mark Kaplan
938. f. U.S. Senate—Scott Skinner
939. a. lieutenant governor—Margaret "Peg" Garland
940. d. attorney general—Bruce Lawlor
941. c. secretary of state—James Douglas

942. b. False. Thomas Salmon carried 13 of 14 against Walter Kennedy in 1974.
943. Peanut
944. c. Philip Hoff—Ralph Foote
945. a. Tom Salmon—John Burgess
946. d. Dick Snelling—Madeleine Kunin
947. b. Madeleine Kunin—Peter Smith
948. a. Yes, in 1964.
949. Naramore
950. St. Michael's
951. Salisbury
952. b. 6
953. In 1912 Vermont joined Utah to vote for Taft, who lost to Wilson.
954. b. Randy Majors.
955. b. Liberty Union
956. d. Citizens Party
957. a. Libertarian
958. c. Small is Beautiful
959. c. Chester Scott
960. a. Elwyn Kernstock
961. d. Tom Evslin
962. b. William G. Craig
963. e. Jim Jeffords
964. a. 27%
965. 3
966. William H. Meyer
967. a. True. The state's share of total state and local highway expenditures from the state's own revenue resources was as follows: 1942 77%; 1957, 67%; 1982, 57%; 1983, 59%; 1984, 65%.
968. b. False. Direct expenditures as a percentage of total personal income ranged between 24% and 25% in 1976 and 1978. In 1983 and 1984 we spent only about 22% of our personal income.
969. Hilton Wick
970. b. a quarter of a million.
971. a. 70%
972. b. 20%
973. c. 8%
974. d. 100%.
975. a. 464.
976. a. True. Our contributions made up 0.18% of the U.S. total.
977. f. Other Taxes—15.9%
978. e. Meals and Rooms Taxes—7.7%
979. b. Income Taxes—38.3%
980. a. Other Revenues—5.5%

981. d. Corporate Taxes—8.4%
982. c. Sales Taxes—24.1%
983. f. Development—1.4%
984. e. Education—43.1%
985. g. Miscellaneous—11.0%
986. a. General—5.9%
987. c. Human Services—28.8%
988. d. Environment—2.2%
989. b. Protection—7.6%

Rank the Vermont political personalities according to their age.

Oldest = 1

990. Madeleine Kunin   ——

991. Richard Snelling   ——

992. Patrick Leahy   ——

993. Peter Smith   ——

994. Philip Hoff   ——

995. Robert Stafford   ——

Youngest = 6

Answers

990. Madeleine Kunin—4 (born 1933)
991. Richard Snelling—3 (born 1927)
992. Patrick Leahy—5 (born 1940)
993. Peter Smith—6 (born 1945)
994. Philip Hoff—2 (born 1924)
995. Robert Stafford—1 (born 1913)

THE FLATLANDER PAGE

At this point in the book, we felt some of you might need a "picker-upper" (so to speak), so we included this. Remember, it is unfair to *try* to get any of these wrong!

How well do you know your common, everyday flatlander terms?

996. _____ Suncountry		a. gym equipment
997. _____ Kettle Brook		b. an inn
998. _____ Tudhope		c. a mall
999. _____ Kiwi		d. a golf course
1000. _____ Telemark		e. hot tubs
1001. _____ Jelly Mill		f. a condo
1002. _____ Calidarium		g. a ski maneuver
1003. _____ Nautilus		h. a drink
1004. _____ Kwiniaska		i. a stove
1005. _____ Resolute		j. yacht sales
1006. _____ Reluctant Panther		k. a fruit

See if you can match the restaurant with the specialty food they feature:

1007. _____ Village Auberge (Dorset)	a. Austrian/German
1008. _____ Jade Wah (Brattleboro)	b. unusual spices
1009. _____ Prince and the Pauper (Woodstock)	c. European cakes
	d. Chinese
1010. _____ Poncho's Wreck (Wilmington)	e. duck
1011. _____ Mainly Yogurt (Bennington)	f. Maine seafood
1012. _____ The Daily Planet (Burlington)	g. Mexican
1013. _____ Patisserie Soigne (Ludlow)	h. salmon mousse
1014. _____ August Lion (Randolph)	i. natural food
1015. _____ Countryman's Pleasure (Mendon)	

1016. *Town and Country* magazine featured two Vermont towns in a July 1986 article entitled "Arcadia in Southern Vermont." It was about the towns of

   a. Woodstock and Pomfret.
   b. Manchester and Dorset.
   c. Stowe and Cambridge.
   d. Hardwick and Wolcott.

The answers to this section begin on page 174.

Where were the following events held in 1985:

1017. _____ 16th Annual Pig Race   a. Killington

1018. _____ Lake Champlain Balloon   b. North Bennington
Festival   c. Stratton

1019. _____ 26th Annual All-Breed
Dog Show and Obedience Trial   d. Goshen
                                     e. Montpelier

1020. _____ Volvo Tennis Tournament   f. Waitsfield

1021. _____ 16th Annual Poetry-in-a-Barn g. Woodstock

1022. _____ 2nd Annual Vermont Fools Fest h. Manchester

1023. _____ Victorian Waltz Ball Weekend i. Shelburne

1024. _____ 6th Annual Garden Party

1025. _____ 4th Annual June 1st Fun
Slalom

1026. Susan Partain-Visen and her husband Barrington Visen III offer a unique service in the Burlington community. With twenty-four hours notice, they will

    a. arrange a lawn party or ski party (depending on season).
    b. serve you breakfast in bed.
    c. bring their portable sauna to your house.
    d. make a home video of you and family or friends.

Answers:
The Flatlander Page

996. h. a drink
997. f. a condo
998. j. yacht sales
999. k. a fruit
1000. g. a ski maneuver
1001. c. a mall
1002. e. hot tubs
1003. a. gym equipment
1004. d. a golf course
1005. i. a stove
1006. b. an inn
1007. e. duck
1008. d. Chinese
1009. h. salmon mousse
1010. g. Mexican
1011. i. natural food
1012. b. unusual spices
1013. c. European cakes
1014. f. Maine seafood
1015. a. Austrian/German
1016. b. Manchester and Dorset. Pictures of beautiful people are captioned by sentences such as: "A stunning European garden provides the perfect luncheon setting for David and Katharine Dickenson, the young Florida couple who bought ex-Wall Streeter Edwin Lefevre's villa, said to be the country's first marble house with, possibly, the first indoor pool." Or how about: "Popular Albany dwellers Michael and Margaret Lindsay Picotte spend their weekends in Vermont. Their log cabin was lovingly built, log by log, by Michael himself. The Picottes are part of the younger crowd that is enlivening the Dorset–Manchester scene."
1017. d. Goshen
1018. i. Shelburne
1019. g. Woodstock
1020. c. Stratton
1021. f. Waitsfield
1022. e. Montpelier
1023. b. North Bennington

1024. h. Manchester
1025. a. Killington
1026. b. You can be served (by a man in a tuxedo) fresh flowers, fresh
croissants, butter, preserves, cheese, fruit, chocolate-covered
truffles, French cider, and a newspaper.

CHAPTER 18

Cow Pie-Throwing Contests and Other Sports

Sport seems entirely estranged from the concept of "Yankee." Yet little Vermont surprises in many ways and we are no exception when it comes to the "thrill of victory and the agony of defeat." There is no area of this book that is less a part of Vermont's self-consciousness than sport. Yet Vermont is positively spiced with sports. We make sport of our work (as in horse-pulling and lumberjack contests) and we excel in those sports that seem natural to our environment, like skiing. Put all that aside, however, and one is still hard put to find an area of Vermont life that provides more variety and innovation than that area of human activity that seeks to rationalize the competitive spirit. Come to think of it, why is that surprising? Vermont was born competitive and life here has always been a competition with the most provocative of opponents, Mother Nature herself.

Big Ten football, be damned! Put Bubba Smith on a pair of wooden slats and tip him over the edge of the National at Stowe or "Doug's Drop" at Burke Mountain and we'll see about nerves and strength and agility and flat-out passion when he hits 65 m.p.h. sans shoulder pads.

But it isn't all like that—as you'll see.

1027. In March of 1986 Floyd Scholz of Hancock, Vermont, "blew the competition out of the water again" according to writer Tom Hill. In Melville, New York, he won 3 blue ribbons in the "national

The answers to Chapter 18 begin on page 184.

championship of an intensely competitive field." What did he do?

a. Rode a horse.
b. Carved an owl.
c. Showed a cow.
d. Paddled a canoe.

1028. About how many snowmobilers in Vermont belong to the Vermont Association of Snow Travelers?

a. 4,000
b. 16,000
c. 24,000

1029. Raymond Roberts of West Fairlee, Vermont, is one of the Northeast's winningest

a. ski jumpers.
b. ox teamsters.
c. amateur runners.
d. water skiers.

1030. Paul LaCross: In 1963 Verner Reed reported of him in *Vermont Life* that "many times challenged, he has never been defeated at the fast draw or in any form of target shooting. And he has met the best of them." His card read "World's fastest, fanciest gunslinger, knife and tomahawk thrower." He did all this from

a. Brattleboro.
b. St. Albans.
c. White River Junction.
d. Rutland.

Match the sport with the sportsperson:

_____	1031. Larry Benoit	a. runner
_____	1032. Gina Sperry	b. horse trainer
_____	1033. Mike Armstrong	c. boxer
_____	1034. Bobby Dragon	d. deer hunter
_____	1035. Cheryl Pratt	e. race-car driver

1036. What do Catamount, Thunder Road, and Bear Ridge all refer to?

On October 5, 1919, (1037.) _____ (player), playing for the (1038.) _____ (team), hit a home run playing against the Rutland baseball team.

177

Match the name of the high-school team with the high school:

_____ 1039. Eagles   a. Otter Valley Union
_____ 1040. Bobwhites   b. Brattleboro
_____ 1041. Marauders   c. Mt. Abraham
_____ 1042. Colonels   d. St. Johnsbury
_____ 1043. Hilltoppers   e. Northfield
_____ 1044. Otters   f. BFA, St. Albans

1045. What do Jade Huntington, Tonia Reed, Wendy Gutzman, and Aija Huntamaki have in common?

Match the sport with the sportsperson:

_____ 1046. Bobby Lefevre   a. kayak racer
_____ 1047. Cindy Paquet   b. ski racer
_____ 1048. Art Wright   c. long-distance ice skater
_____ 1049. Docke Dam   d. golfer
_____ 1050. Tiger Shaw   e. boxer
_____ 1051. Terry White   f. big-game hunter

He won (1052.) _____ New England heavyweight Golden Gloves tournaments in a row, the only person in modern history to do so. He was the first Vermonter ever to win even (1053.) _____ New England championships. In 1980 he won 3 fights in the national championships and lost in the semifinals. A native of (1054.) _____, he was the 1975 Vermont schoolboy discus and shotput champ. It is hard to name another Vermonter in recent times that has so distinguished himself in what has not been a traditional Vermont sport. Don Fillion says of him: "He should go down in history as perhaps the best Golden Gloves boxer in Vermont history." His name: (1055.) _____.

Match the coaches with the sports they are best known for:

_____ 1056. Ed Markey   a. schoolboy football
_____ 1057. Sheila Bruleigh   b. basketball (college)
_____ 1058. Mike Gallagher   c. baseball
_____ 1059. Ralph Lapointe   d. boxing
_____ 1060. Red Gendron   e. cross-country skiing
_____ 1061. Denis E. Lambert   f. hockey
_____ 1062. Dr. Donald Veburst   g. basketball (high school)

In the 1950's a basketball team from Vermont became a national contender. The team was known as the (1063.) _____ Knights. They represented (1064.) _____ College and were coached by (1065.) _____.

1066. When Thunder Road is filled to capacity, it seats about

    a. 4,000.
    b. 8,000.
    c. 12,000.
    d. 16,000.

1067. What do these 5 men all have in common?

Henry Augustoni
Verge Smith
Steve Ferreira
Spencer Noble
Daryl "Squirrel" Sawyer

1068. The record crowd at Milton's Catamount Stadium on June 29, 1985, was about

    a. 7,000 people.
    b. 11,000 people.
    c. 15,000 people.

1069. Southeastern Vermont, especially Putney, has been the home of world-class athletes in this sport for years. They have put America on the map in a sport long dominated by Europeans. What is it?

1070. In the 1984 Winter Olympics, Vermont had more members of the U.S. team than any other state.

    a. True
    b. False

1071. One of America's best-known sportscasters and *the* most recognized in auto racing (because of his association with CBS) worked for years at "The Voice of Vermont," WDEV in Waterbury. His name is _____.

1072. One out of every _____ Vermonters (men, women, and children) belongs to a bowling league.

    a. 25
    b. 50
    c. 100
    d. 500

1073. Cornell University's all-time scoring leader in basketball graduated from Oxbow High School.

a. True
b. False

1074. Vermont's best-known T.V. sportscaster began at WCAX radio in 1951 and moved to channel three in 1954. Who is he?

The "voices" of two American League baseball teams both have backgrounds in Vermont broadcasting.

The Boston Red Sox's (1075.) _____, who worked at a radio station in (1076.) _____ (city) in Vermont.

The Toronto Blue Jay's (1077.) _____, who worked at a radio station in (1078.) _____ (city) in Vermont.

1079. The Phantoms and Ghosts are both _____ teams.

    a. professional soaring
    b. college soccer
    c. schoolgirl basketball
    d. men's polo

1080. From Brattleboro, he won the Vermont Amateur Men's Golfing tournament in 1983 and 1985. Who is he?

1081. Stamford, Vermont, has a unique sporting facility. What is it?

    a. A bobsled run that ends in a lake.
    b. A baseball diamond with no second base.
    c. A 7-hole golf course.
    d. A race track with no finish line.

1082. A "Flying Tiger" is a kind of competition in what sport?

Every year in Barre there is held the (1083.) "_____ Bowl" Late-Model Stock Car Race. The winner kisses a (1084.) _____ and the event is preceded by a (1085.) _____ contest.

The first American medal in Olympic Nordic skiing was won by (1086.) _____ of (1087.) _____, Vermont, in the year (1088.) _____.

The first Olympic gold medals ever awarded to a woman in skiing were won by Andrea (1089.) _____ of (1090.) _____, Vermont, in 1952.

180

1091. In 1976, Tad Coffin of Strafford won the first American gold medal ever in what sport?

    a. Ski jumping
    b. Horseback riding
    c. Fencing
    d. Pole-vaulting

1092. A graduate of a Vermont high school was a starter on the number one-ranked Division I NCAA College Basketball team in 1986.

    a. True
    b. False

1093. In 1972 she won an Olympic gold medal in the slalom. Her name is?

Match the team with the school it represents:

_____	1094. Cosmos	a. Hartford
_____	1095. Little Indians	b. Mt. St. Joseph's, Rutland
_____	1096. Thunderbirds	c. Mill River
_____	1097. Hurricanes	d. Rice, Burlington
_____	1098. Indians	e. Danville
_____	1099. Mounties	f. Oxbow, Bradford/Newbury
_____	1100. Olympians	g. Springfield
_____	1101. Minutemen	h. Missisquoi

Billy Kidd was a (1102.) _____ from (1103.) _____.
He won a (1104.) _____ medal in the (1105.) _____ Olympics.

Match the sportsperson with the sport:

_____	1106. Bill McGill	a. cross-country skiing
_____	1107. John Trotier	b. sled dog racing
_____	1108. Betsy Snite	c. ski racing
_____	1109. William Carow	d. biathlon
_____	1110. Jennifer Caldwell	e. horse-pulling

The Great Santini of Vermont Sports

He is known as one of the feistiest players ever to play sports in Vermont.

When he graduated from Bradford Academy in 1959, he was Vermont's best schoolboy athlete. In basketball, his 47 points set a record

181

that lasted over 20 years for most points in a tournament game. In 4 years at Bradford he scored 1,960 points, another record that lasted over 20 years. He took Bradford to the state championship in 1959. In a low scoring game (44–38) he scored 26, shooting 70% from the floor and 12 of 13 from the line. With time running out in the fourth quarter and his team behind, a time-out was called. When he returned to the floor, there were 62 seconds left in his high-school career. Clutch City. He stole the ball 3 times, scored a jumper, 3 foul shots, and made a crisp feed under the basket to win it for Bradford.

But his best sport was baseball. The Milwaukee Braves signed him (with a bonus) to play for them in 1959. He was a catcher. At 5 feet 9 inches and 145 pounds, he was all guts and muscle and skill and determination. He also had a raw, flat-out craze to win. But you've got to weigh more than 145 to catch in the majors. He came back to Bradford and married his high-school sweetheart, Donna Drew, a former cheerleader.

Their children are cutting a wide swath in Vermont sports. His son Ron was a Vermont standout in 3 sports: baseball, soccer, and basketball. The Vermont record for most points scored in soccer in 4 years is still his. He played league-leading baseball in college in North Carolina under former UVM coach Jack Leggett. The Braves drafted him in 1986. His other son, Randy, beat out a key hit at the 1982 state championship baseball game which Bradford won over Winooski in 18 innings. (In that same game, other son Ron hit a home run well out of the park at Centennial Field and pitched 10 innings of *relief*—after playing 8 innings at short stop.) Kevin Iole described Randy's play in a key basketball game against Lamoille in the 1984 State Tournament this way: With time running out, he "put on a clinic . . . twisting and bending his body into more positions than a limbo artist in the process." Shades of his father. As a sophomore at Oxbow (the union school that now includes Bradford), his daughter Jade was the best schoolgirl basketball player in Vermont in 1986. At 5 feet 5 inches, she was selected a first team All-American in the Junior Olympics at Kansas City. And there is another one, Jasmyne, to come. She was 9 in 1986 and for her age she is bigger, taller, and stronger.

He was a player in the Vermont tradition. His deadly jump shot had no arc. Copying from Eddie Steel of Waterbury, he learned to gun it in under the rafters in his father's barn. There was none better in Vermont in the late 1950's. He ran home from practice to do chores in that same barn. He knew cows. Pound for pound it is hard to name a better all-around athlete to come out of a Vermont high school since World War II.

Vince Lombardi would have loved him because he can't *stand* to lose. He just can't. He hates to see his team lose, his town lose, his friends lose, his kids lose. His competitive spirit is still awesome. In the past that spirit carried him into the zone of "questionable behavior." It is the penalty for being a warrior without a war—to be on the sidelines while every atom in you craves action. Yet the people of Bradford know that a kid with a baseball that walks up to him and says "let's throw a few" or "teach me how to catch" will get his wish. He'll give his time, his spirit. He'll give himself. He always has. He is the Great Santini of Vermont sports. His name is (1111.) ————————————————.

1112. Who is this man? ——————————

Photo from Sports Information at the University of Vermont

Answers:
Cow Pie-Throwing Contests and Other Sports

1027. b. Carved an owl in the National Decoy and Bird Carvers Show.
1028. b. 16,000
1029. b. ox teamsters.
1030. b. St. Albans.
1031. d. Larry Benoit of Duxbury is to Vermont deer hunting what Ali was to boxing. Over the past 30 years he has shot 30 deer that have weighed over 200 pounds.
1032. a. In the spring of 1986, Sperry (of South Burlington) won half a million dollars in a race on ABC's Wide World of Sports.
1033. c. Mike Armstrong is a boxer.
1034. e. Bobby Dragon is a race-car driver.
1035. b. Cheryl Pratt is a horse trainer.
1036. Race tracks in Milton, Barre, and Bradford.
1037. Babe Ruth
1038. Boston Red Sox
1039. c. Mt. Abraham Eagles
1040. f. BFA Bobwhites
1041. e. Northfield Marauders
1042. b. Brattleboro Colonels
1043. d. St. Johnsbury Hilltoppers
1044. a. Otter Valley Otters
1045. They all play schoolgirl basketball.
1046. e. Bobby Lefevre was one of Vermont's best amateur fighters in the lighter divisions in the 1950's and early 1960's.
1047. d. Cindy Paquet is a 5-time winner of the Vermont Women's State Amateur Golf Tournament.
1048. f. Art Wright is a big-game hunter. You should see his trophy room.
1049. c. A Panton dairy farmer, this man is a veteran long-distance skater who has competed in the longest races in the world. He once almost lost a finger when he fell and was run over by another skater.
1050. b. With a name like that, Shaw *has* to be a ski racer.
1051. a. A 1983 silver medalist in Holland, Terry White dominated U.S. kayak racing in the early 1980's.
1052. 4
1053. 2
1054. Newport

184

1055. Tony Robitaille. (Who says country boys can't fight!).

1056. b. Ed Markey—basketball (college)

1057. g. Sheila Bruleigh—basketball (high school)

1058. e. Mike Gallagher—cross country skiing

1059. c. Ralph Lapointe—baseball

1060. f. Red Gendron—hockey

1061. a. Denis E. Lambert—schoolboy football

1062. d. Dr. Donald Veburst—boxing

1063. Iron. (Because the 5 starters played so much of each game. The team is commonly known as the "Purple Knights.")

1064. St. Michael's

1065. Doc Jacobs

1066. c. 12,000 (2,500 in the bleachers, 9,500 on the grass).

1067. They are all referees in Vermont high-school basketball.

1068. b. 11,000 people.

1069. Nordic skiing

1070. a. True

1071. Ken Squires

1072. a. 25

1073. a. True. Karen Dwyer is known as one of the best basketball players in the Ivy League.

1074. Tony Adams

1075. Ken Coleman

1076. Rutland

1077. Tom Cheek

1078. Burlington

1079. c. schoolgirl basketball. The Ghosts are from Randolph and the Phantoms are from Proctor. Do they have seances before practice?

1080. Shawn Baker

1081. c. A 7-hole golf course

1082. Automobile racing

1083. Milk

1084. cow

1085. cow pie-throwing

1086. Bill Koch

1087. Guilford. Incidentally, the residents of Guilford were threatened as follows by Ethan Allen during the "Guilford War." "I, Ethan Allen, do declare that I will give no quarter to any man, woman, or child, who shall oppose me, and unless the inhabitants of Guilford peacefully submit to the authority of Vermont, I swear I will lay it as desolate as Sodom and Gomorrah, by God!" What had the Guilford people done? They had ambushed Allen and, according to historian Earle Newton, caused him to "beat a hasty and undignified retreat." Much in the same manner, Koch ambushed the world of Nordic ski racers 2 centuries later.

1088. 1976. It was a silver medal in the 30-kilometer race.

1089. Mead

1090. Rutland

1091. b. Flatlanders call it "equestrian" something or other.

1092. b. False. Bruce Dalrymple of St. Johnsbury Academy did start for number one Georgia Tech. But they ranked number one before the season began and lost this ranking after their first game. They were never ranked number one in 1986.

1093. Barbara Cochran

1094. g. Springfield Cosmos

1095. d. Rice Little Indians

1096. h. Missisquoi Thunderbirds

1097. a. Hartford Hurricanes

1098. e. Danville Indians

1099. b. Mt. St. Joseph Mounties

1100. f. Oxbow Olympians

1101. c. Mill River Minutemen

1102. ski racer

1103. Stowe

1104. silver

1105. 1964

1106. e. Bill McGill—horse pulling

1107. b. John Trotier—sled dog racing

1108. c. Betsy Snite—ski racing

1109. d. William Carow—biathlon

1110. a. Jennifer Caldwell—cross country skiing

1111. George "Tootie" Huntington

1112. He is Vermont's best-ever baseball player. Babe Ruth called him the best third baseman he'd ever seen. Ty Cobb said he was "the best third baseman I ever played against." He was a native Vermonter from Enosburg Falls. A chemistry major, he graduated from UVM in 1909—one of the first professional baseball players with a college education. He played for the Boston Red Sox, and he's in the Baseball Hall of Fame. His name is Larry Gardner.

1113.

What is Vermont's "Best-Kept Secret"?

Answer

"Vermont's Best-Kept Secret" is the slogan used by the Newport Chamber of Commerce to advertise the beautiful Lake Memphremagog country. There is a certain dignity that accents the natural and even awesome beauty of Vermont's most northern city and the people who live, as Bob Dylan and Johnny Cash say in a folksong, "where the winds hit heavy on the borderline."

CHAPTER 19

What Do You *Do* Up There?

Every Vermonter who has traveled out of state has probably heard something like this: "Yes I know it's beautiful, but what do you *do* up there?" If you find it hard to answer this question, we think that's proof you are in love with Vermont. Real lovers don't have time to ponder the question. It is with some trepidation, therefore, that we approach this chapter. Yet, not counting the hundreds of natural pleasures like hiking, fishing, "looking for deer," and just "being," or the more structured activities like skiing or boating, it is still amazing to discover the number of "things to do" in Vermont.

1114. If you were going to Weston, Vermont, for a summer evening's entertainment, you would probably be going to the

_____.

1115. Clock Works in Ludlow is a

    a. ski shop.
    b. restaurant.
    c. clock shop.
    d. museum.

1116. The Good Time Shoppe in Woodstock is a

    a. house of ill repute.
    b. deli.
    c. clock shop.
    d. vintage clothing store.

The answers to Chapter 19 begin on page 194.

1117. Which three of the following popular places are restaurants?

   a. Forlie-Ballou in Chester
   b. Hemingway's in Killington
   c. Yankee Pride in Winooski
   d. Casey's Caboose in Killington
   e. Season's Best in Rutland
   f. Blackfriar in Bennington
   g. One Bond Street in Woodstock

1118. To celebrate its Fiftieth Anniversary, the Vermont Symphony Orchestra launched a successful "251 Project." What was it?

1119. Spell the name of the large Burlington hotel that overlooks Lake Champlain.

Below are listed pairs of events that occurred in 1985 in Vermont. Match them with the month of the year in which they occurred.

   a. January   g. July
   b. February   h. August
   c. March   i. September
   d. April   j. October
   e. May   k. November
   f. June   l. December

_____ 1120. The 33rd Annual Cracker Barrel Bazaar, Newbury
            The 17th Annual Fiddler's Contest, Calais

_____ 1121. The Tunbridge Fair, Tunbridge
            25th Annual Dowsing Convention, Danville

_____ 1122. Snowmobile Drag Races, Springfield
            Ice Harvest, Brookfield

_____ 1123. Bennington County Horse Show, Manchester
            The 6th Annual Lilac Sunday Celebration, Shelburne
              Museum, Shelburne

_____ 1124. The 3rd Annual First Night, Burlington
            Candlelight Tours, Manchester

_____ 1125. 29th Annual Wild Game Supper, Bradford
            14th Annual Craft Fair, Jericho Corners

_____ 1126. 29th Annual Winter Carnival, Brattleboro
            1st New England Sled Dog Races, Waitsfield

_____ 1127. The 10th Annual Rotten Sneaker Contest, Montpelier
            Home/Leisure Show, Bellows Falls

_____ 1128. 15th Annual Heritage Festival, Newfane
13th Annual Vermont Bird Conference, Woodstock

_____ 1129. 11th Annual Canoe-A-Thon, Newport
27th Annual Fire Department Turkey Dinner, Starksboro

_____ 1130. 13th Anniversary Art Show, East Burke
6th Annual Family Festival, Hyde Park

_____ 1131. Maple Festival, St. Albans
Ottauquechee River Raft Race, Woodstock

Find the town that hosted each of the following fairs and festivals in 1985.

_____ 1132. Addison County Field Days   a. East Burke
_____ 1133. Vermont Apple Festival   b. Essex Junction
_____ 1134. Champlain Valley Exposition   c. New Haven
_____ 1135. Deerfield Valley Farmers Days   d. Quechee
_____ 1136. 4–H State Dairy Days   e. Rutland
_____ 1137. Harvest Festival   f. Shelburne
_____ 1138. Hot Air Balloon Festival   g. South Burlington
_____ 1139. Sheep and Wool Festival   h. Springfield
_____ 1140. Annual Labor Day Weekend   i. Guilford
Festival   j. Tunbridge
_____ 1141. Vermont State Fair   k. Wilmington
_____ 1142. World's Fair

1143. The Highland Lodge and Willey's Store are found on what lake in northern Vermont?

    a. Willoughby
    b. Memphremagog
    c. Caspian
    d. Seymour

1144. The Colatina Exit is

    a. an Italian restaurant in Bradford.
    b. an exit off I–89 in Colchester.
    c. a novice ski trail at Stowe.
    d. an antique shop in Woodstock.

1145. What does The Real Scoop in Bellows Falls specialize in?

1146. The Huntington House, a restored 1806 house with guest rooms and restaurant, is situated in

a. Shelburne.

b. Huntington.

c. Rochester.

d. Bethel.

1147. If you stopped at the Water Works in Waitsfield, you might be apt to

a. have a drink with friends.

b. take a dip in a hot tub.

c. purchase a sink.

d. have your car washed.

1148. There is a restaurant in Manchester housed in a six-sided building. It is called

a. The Manchester Six.

b. Half a Dozen.

c. Double Hex.

d. 3 Plus 3.

1149. T.J. Buckley's restaurant in Brattleboro was once a

a. train station.

b. school.

c. barn.

d. church.

1150. On the last weekend in August thousands of people go to Glover to witness

a. the Bread and Puppet Theatre Convention.

b. the Northern Highlands Festival.

c. the Domestic Resurrection Circus.

d. the Green Mountain Jamboree.

1151. Whiskers is the name of a

a. pet store in Shelburne.

b. barber shop in Bennington.

c. restaurant in Stowe.

d. men's store in Winooski.

1152. Memphremagog International Aquafest is a swim race held in July which begins in the town of _____ and ends in Magog in Canada.

1153. On October 7, 1985, Governor Kunin proclaimed the beginning of

    a. Vermont Apple Week.
    b. Vermont Farm Week.
    c. Vermont Maple Week.
    d. Vermont Foliage Week.

1154. What popular Burlington restaurant has a menu that is thirty pages long?

1155. At the "Stowe Marathon" in tiny Moscow, Vermont, the participants parade to music from

    a. the elementary school band.
    b. radios.
    c. singers.
    d. a taped recording.

1156. In which of the following would you be unable to order a pepperoni pizza in the Burlington area?

    a. Big Ben's
    b. Mr. Mike's
    c. Francesca's
    d. Zachary's

1157. Four Winds, Cassie Sioux, and Room for One More are all Vermont

    a. tennis clubs.
    b. riding stables.
    c. golf courses.
    d. playhouses.

1158. *Yankee* Magazine's 1985 Travel Guide to New England rated Mary's their favorite restaurant in Vermont. You can dine at this fascinating spot by traveling to

    a. Bellows Falls.
    b. Bennington.
    c. Bristol.
    d. Burlington.

1159. In 1980, Governor Tom's entered the dining scene in Waterbury Center. For whom is it named?

1160. On October 14, 1985, Stratton Mountain was the scene of the

    a. 1st Annual Stratton Arts Festival.
    b. 22nd Annual Stratton Arts Festival.
    c. 100th Annual Stratton Arts Festival.

1161. The name of the gift shop/country store/museum housed in a 160-year-old authentic Vermont barn in St. Johnsbury is

    a. the Farmer's Barn.
    b. Chore Time.
    c. the Farmer's Daughter.
    d. the Hayloft Museum.

1162. What do the following have in common?

The Bread and Puppet in Glover
The American Precision in Windsor
The Kent Tavern in Calais
The Peter Matterson Tavern in Shaftsbury

1163. One of Vermont's better-known restaurants is in Strafford, Vermont. It is called the _____ Soup.

1164. Which one does not fit?

    a. J-Stroke
    b. Undercut
    c. Cross Draw
    d. Inverted Sweep

Answers:
What Do You *Do* Up There?

1114. Weston Playhouse
1115. b. A full-service restaurant named for the new clock tower at Okemo's entrance.
1116. c. A clock shop, of course.
1117. b, d, and f are restaurants.
    a. is a women's specialty shop.
    c. sells quilts.
    e. is a women's clothing store.
    g. sells gentlemen's clothing.
1118. A project to send their musicians to perform in each of Vermont's cities and towns.
1119. R-A-D-I-S-S-O-N
1120. g. July
1121. i. September
1122. a. January
1123. e. May
1124. l. December
1125. k. November
1126. b. February
1127. c. March
1128. j. October
1129. f. June
1130. h. August
1131. d. April
1132. c. New Haven
1133. h. Springfield
1134. b. Essex Junction
1135. k. Wilmington
1136. g. South Burlington
1137. f. Shelburne
1138. d. Quechee
1139. a. East Burke
1140. i. Guilford
1141. e. Rutland
1142. j. Tunbridge
1143. c. Caspian
1144. a. (You didn't pick b, did you?)
1145. Ice cream. Get it?
1146. c. Rochester.

1147. b. take a dip in a hot tub.

1148. c. Double Hex.

1149. d. church.

1150. c. Held on the Bread and Puppet Theatre's farm, the Domestic Resurrection Circus includes a "circus" of giant puppets on stilts. Free homemade bread is distributed.

1151. c. restaurant in Stowe.

1152. Newport

1153. a. Vermont Apple Week.

1154. Carbur's. And their menu is called the Encycloeatia Carburanica.

1155. b. radios.

1156. c. At Francesca's the cuisine is Italian but instead of pizza you would find such things as Fritto di Fontina, Pesce Fume, Calamari Friti, and Fresh Ravioli.

1157. b. riding stables. Four Winds Farm is in Barre, Cassie Sioux Stables is in South Starksboro, and Room for One More Ranch is in Randolph.

1158. c. Main Street, Bristol.

1159. Thomas Chittenden, governor of Vermont 1778–1797.

1160. b. Established in 1964, it is the largest showcase for work of Vermont painters, craftsmen, photographers, and sculptors.

1161. c. the Farmer's Daughter.

1162. They are all museums.

1163. Stone

1164. b. The Undercut is not a canoe stroke.

1165.

One of Vermont's most famous foul-ups is found in the town of Cambridge. What is it?

Answer

The bridge across the Lamoille River was actually built *backwards!*

CHAPTER 20

Old Ruggedness, New Softness*
Vermont's Geography

Perhaps one reason why Vermont is so unique is that the linkage between people and place—its geography—is so clear. Vermont is a land of ups and downs, hill and dale, nooks and crannies. Its hundreds of rivers and streams have cut and rounded (and even flattened here and there) places for us to live. These are small places, quiet places, *natural* places. Before the bulldozer was discovered that was how it, blessedly, had to be. Whereas before we put our houses where the land was right, now we put the land where the houses will be right. And sooner or later we'll pay for it!

1166. How long is Vermont?

   a. About 100 miles
   b. About 150 miles
   c. About 250 miles
   d. About 300 miles

1167. The Connecticut River belongs to

   a. Connecticut.
   b. New Hampshire.
   c. Vermont.
   d. Vermont and New Hampshire jointly.

*Charles W. Johnson describes Vermont in his *Nature of Vermont* as follows: "Vermont is modestly grand, a softness over old ruggedness, blessed with diversity of land and wildlife."

The answers to Chapter 20 begin on page 203.

196

1168. How big is the Northeast Kingdom?

    a. 600 square miles
    b. 2,000 square miles
    c. 5,000 square miles
    d. 10,000 square miles

1169. Interstate 89 extends all the way from New Hampshire to Canada. The highest point on this highway is

    a. north of Sharon, south of Montpelier.
    b. south of Sharon.
    c. north of Montpelier, south of St. Albans.
    d. north of St. Albans.

1170. You are driving south on I–89 and you have just passed the exit for Sharon. The next large river you cross is the

    a. Black River.
    b. White River.
    c. Connecticut River.
    d. Winooski River.

1171. Vermont is the only New England state without a coastline.

    a. True
    b. False

1172. Three rivers—the Passumpsic, Moose, and Sleepers—meet in what town?

The islands that extend south from the Canadian border into Lake Champlain and make up Vermont's Grand Isle County consist of what 5 towns?

1173. _____, 1174. _____, 1175. _____, 1176. _____, and 1177. _____.

1178. Montpelier was named for a small city in

    a. New York.
    b. Moldavia.
    c. France.
    d. England.

1179. Of the following, which town is the northernmost?

a. Morgan
b. St. Albans
c. Newport
d. Lowell

1180. Of the following, which is the southernmost?

a. Vernon
b. Brattleboro
c. Bennington
d. Wilmington

1181. Which town does not border on the Connecticut River?

a. Windsor
b. Westminster
c. Norwich
d. Groton

On the map on the opposite page locate the following and place the correct letter by the number of the question:

_____ 1182. Camel's Hump

_____ 1183. Montpelier

_____ 1184. Rutland City

_____ 1185. The Lamoille River

_____ 1186. Stowe

_____ 1187. Jay Peak

_____ 1188. Hazen's Notch

_____ 1189. Johnson State College

_____ 1190. Burke Mountain

_____ 1191. Middlebury College

_____ 1192. Victory Bog

_____ 1193. The West River

_____ 1194. Mt. Equinox

_____ 1195. St. Albans

_____ 1196. The Batten Kill River

_____ 1197. Hunger Mountain

_____ 1198. Ludlow

_____ 1199. Otter Creek

1200. Pick out the 2 towns in Orleans County.

a. Barton
b. Enosburg
c. Norton
d. Glover

1201. I–89 does not pass through one of these. Which one?

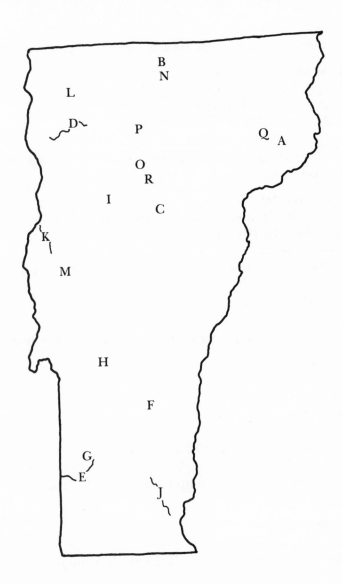

a. Montpelier
b. Waterbury
c. St. Albans
d. Essex Junction

1202. Which one is not a "gore"?

a. Avery
b. Warren
c. Buels
d. Lewis

1203. What does the Indian name for Champlain, "Petonbowk," mean?

    a. Lake of Shining Waters
    b. Waters Long and Blue
    c. Waters that Lie Between
    d. Lake of the Abenaki Nation

1204. If you were to walk around the entire shoreline of Lake Champlain, you would

    a. walk over 500 miles.
    b. be walking around the largest fresh water lake in the U.S. excluding the Great Lakes.
    c. both of the above.
    d. neither of the above.

1205. What river is the state capital on?

1206. Of the following places, which one borders on Lake Champlain?

    a. Winooski
    b. Swanton
    c. Sheldon
    d. Waltham

1207. Which direction does Lake Champlain flow?

1208. Which is the biggest lake completely within the state's border?

    a. Bomoseen
    b. Seymour
    c. Carmi
    d. Harriman Reservoir (also called Lake Whitingham)

1209. Where is 15-Mile Falls?

1210. Which extends further south, Rutland County or Windsor County?

1211. Ticklenaked Pond is in the town of

    a. Groton.
    b. Ryegate.
    c. Clarendon.
    d. Newport.

1212. In the town of Newbury the Connecticut River forms great shapes

in the land that have been named the big and little
_____.

1213. Where did the Runaway Pond runaway?

Match the river with the body of water it flows into. (Each body of water gets two rivers.)

River	Body of Water
_____ 1214. The Batten Kill	a. Lake Memphremagog
_____ 1215. The Clyde	b. Lake Champlain
_____ 1216. The Lamoille	c. The Connecticut River
_____ 1217. The Nulhegan	d. The Hudson River
_____ 1218. The West	
_____ 1219. The Winooski	
_____ 1220. The Hoosic	
_____ 1221. The Barton	

1222. Which river marks the fall line of the Connecticut River?

1223. One of Vermont's lakes has an Indian name that means "Beautiful Waters." It is

    a. Ninevah.
    b. Winnipesaukee.
    c. Memphremagog.
    d. Willoughby.

1224. What is the pond in the Northeast Kingdom that is named after and shaped like a continent?

Match the town on the left with one on the right that borders it to the east:

_____ 1225. Rupert	a. Guilford
_____ 1226. Fairfax	b. Fairfax
_____ 1227. Georgia	c. Sutton
_____ 1228. Halifax	d. Dorset
_____ 1229. Sheffield	e. Fletcher

1230. Which town is closest to the center of the state?

    a. Ludlow
    b. Randolph
    c. Moretown
    d. Stockbridge

1231. According to physical size, which Vermont town is the largest?

    a. Stowe
    b. Chittenden
    c. Cambridge
    d. Newbury

1232. The smallest town according to physical size is

    a. Baltimore.
    b. Waltham.
    c. St. George.
    d. Whiting.

There are actually 4 rivers in the White River system. Match the river with the town of its source:

_____ 1233. White	a. Washington
_____ 1234. East Branch	b. Roxbury
_____ 1235. Second Branch	c. Ripton
_____ 1236. Third Branch	d. Williamstown

Match the following rivers with their town of origin:

_____ 1237. Lamoille	a. Mt. Holly
_____ 1238. Ompompanoosuc	b. Dorset
_____ 1239. Otter Creek	c. Greensboro
_____ 1240. Passumpsic	d. Vershire
_____ 1241. West	e. Westmore

1242. What do the following towns and cities have in common?

    Guildhall
    Burlington
    Hyde Park
    Newfane
    Chelsea

Answers:
Old Ruggedness, New Softness

1166. b. 151.5 miles to be exact.
1167. b. New Hampshire.
1168. b. 2,000 square miles
1169. a. north of Sharon, south of Montpelier.
1170. b. White River.
1171. a. True
1172. St. Johnsbury
1173. Isle La Motte (1173–1177 can be in any order)
1174. North Hero
1175. Alburg
1176. Grand Isle
1177. South Hero
1178. c. France.
1179. c. Newport
1180. a. Vernon
1181. d. Groton
1182. i. Camel's Hump
1183. c. Montpelier
1184. h. Rutland City
1185. d. The Lamoille River
1186. o. Stowe
1187. b. Jay Peak
1188. n. Hazen's Notch
1189. p. Johnson State College
1190. q. Burke Mountain
1191. m. Middlebury College
1192. a. Victory Bog
1193. j. The West River
1194. g. Mt. Equinox
1195. l. St. Albans
1196. e. The Batten Kill River
1197. r. Hunger Mountain
1198. f. Ludlow
1199. k. Otter Creek
1200. a. & d. Barton and Glover
1201. d. Essex Junction
1202. d. Lewis
1203. c. Waters that Lie Between
1204. c. both of the above.

1205. The Winooski River

1206. b. Swanton

1207. North

1208. d. Harriman Reservoir with 2,496 acres. If you answered Bomoseen with 2,395 acres, call it close enough. (Carmi in Franklin has 1,417 acres and Seymour in Morgan has 1,723 acres.)

1209. Barnet

1210. Windsor County

1211. b. Ryegate.

1212. oxbows

1213. Glover

1214. d. Hudson River

1215. a. Lake Memphremagog

1216. b. Lake Champlain

1217. c. Connecticut River

1218. c. Connecticut River

1219. b. Lake Champlain

1220. d. Hudson River

1221. a. Lake Memphremagog

1222. The Wells River. In 1830 a steamer actually reached the Wells River from Hartford, Connecticut.

1223. c. Memphremagog (of course you knew that Winnipesaukee is in New Hampshire!).

1224. South America Pond in Ferdinand

1225. d. Rupert—Dorset

1226. e. Fairfax—Fletcher

1227. b. Georgia—Fairfax

1228. a. Halifax—Guilford

1229. c. Sheffield—Sutton

1230. b. Randolph

1231. b. Chittenden with 46,315 acres.

1232. c. St. George with 2,184 acres.

1233. c. White—Ripton

1234. a. East Branch—Washington

1235. d. Second Branch—Williamstown

1236. b. Third Branch—Roxbury

1237. c. Lamoille—Greensboro

1238. d. Ompompanoosuc—Vershire

1239. b. Otter Creek—Dorset

1240. e. Passumpsic—Westmore

1241. a. West—Mt. Holly

1242. They are all the shire towns of their county.

1243.

Of the following Vermont counties, which one grew the fastest between 1970 and 1980?

>   a. Chittenden
>   b. Bennington
>   c. Grand Isle
>   d. Windsor

Answer

c. Grand Isle County grew the fastest.

THE PRESIDENTIAL PAGE

Summer people, flatlanders, city folks, and other assorted varieties of "non-Vermonter" status must get sick of the boast, "But did you know that Vermont's tiny population actually produced *two* Presidents of the United States?" Too bad. Did you know that Vermont's tiny population actually produced two Presidents of the United States?

1244. The Republican campaign slogan of 1924 was "Keep _____ and Keep Coolidge."

1245. Who was the Democrat Coolidge defeated in 1924?

    a. John W. Davis
    b. James M. Cox
    c. Alfred E. Smith

1246. Which of the following is *not* true about Chester Arthur and Calvin Coolidge?

    a. Both were lawyers.
    b. Both served as governors of other states.
    c. Both were Republicans.
    d. Both became president because an incumbent president died.

Link the items on the left with the president to whom it most clearly applies:

	Arthur	*Coolidge*
1247. They called him "Gentleman Boss"	_____	_____
1248. Was a general in the Civil War	_____	_____
1249. "How can they tell?"	_____	_____
1250. Civil service reform	_____	_____
1251. Police strike in Boston	_____	_____
1252. "The business of America is business"	_____	_____

The answers to this section begin on page 208.

	Arthur	Coolidge
1253. Was a widower in the White House	————	————
1254. Attended Amherst College	————	————
1255. Was given the oath of office in Vermont	————	————

1256. James Garfield (20th president) and Chester Arthur (Garfield's vice president and 21st president) had a Vermont connection before they served together. What was it?

a. They were both born in Vermont.
b. They both attended college in Vermont.
c. They both taught at the same academy in Vermont.
d. They both married women from Vermont.

1257. Townshend, Vermont, is known for its linkage to a great American political family in Ohio that produced President

————————.

Answers:
The Presidential Page

1244. "Keep <u>Cool</u> and Keep Coolidge."
1245. a. John W. Davis
1246. b. Both served as governors of other states. (Only Coolidge did.)
1247. Arthur. He was strongly connected with Roscoe Conkling's political machine in New York. He was also known as the perfect gentleman and entertainer. One admirer said of him: "It is not that he is handsome and agreeable—for he was both long ago, but it is his ease, polish and perfect manner that make him the greatest society lion we have had in many years."
1248. Arthur
1249. When Dorothy Parker was told that Coolidge was dead, she exclaimed, "How can they tell?"
1250. Arthur was a supporter of Garfield's innovations in civil service reform. Roscoe Conkling, displeased with Arthur's change of perspective when he became president, called it "snivel service" reform.
1251. When governor of Massachusetts, Coolidge gained national attention for his famous statement: "There is no right to strike against the public safety by anybody, anywhere, anytime."
1252. This is another famous Coolidge remark.
1253. Arthur. His sister was hostess in the White House.
1254. Coolidge.
1255. Coolidge. When word of Harding's death reached him, his father, a notary public, swore him in in his parlor by kerosene lamp.
1256. c. Arthur taught in North Pownal, Vermont, three years before Garfield taught there.
1257. William H. Taft. Morrissey in *Vermont: A History* reports that Alphonso Taft remarked to his father in 1837 that Vermont was "a noble state to emigrate from" when he "decided to part from Townshend and cast his future as the first of the Tafts to prosper in the bustling Ohio River town of Cincinnati."

CHAPTER 21

The Category Is Vermont

We don't know if either Alex Trebek or Art Fleming are Vermont-ers. But anyone who has watched "Jeopardy" in Vermont (on TV stations from out-of-state that broadcast NBC) must have noticed that Vermont turns up quite often as an "answer." Here is a pure Vermont version of America's favorite real* quiz show. (For those of you who don't know how to play, below are answers. Your job: supply the questions to them.)

Single Jeopardy

1258. The state beverage.

1259. The set of strict land-use laws passed in 1970.

1260. The Reds.

1261. Sugar on snow.

1262. The honeybee.

1263. Twelve days before Thanksgiving.

1264. The state horse.

1265. Champ.

1266. Eight-zero-two

1267. Hermit thrush.

*As opposed to programs like "The Price is Right" or "Wheel of Fortune."

The answers to Chapter 21 begin on page 212.

1268. The WCAX-TV farm and home show hosted by Tony Adams.

1269. The Bennington Mob.

1270. The world's largest granite quarry.

1271. Vermont's fifth season.

1272. DING, DING, DING—A DAILY DOUBLE

This is a Visual Daily Double

1272.   The statue marks the junction of Routes 302 and 14 in this town.

Double Jeopardy

1273.   "The Smallest City in the USA."

1274.   The highest grade of maple syrup.

1275.   Suicide Six.

1276.   "I had a lover's quarrel with the world."

1277.   A hydrometer.

1278.   Brattleboro, Dover, Stratton, and Westminster, for example.

1279.   "Peaceful she lies, but when roused to a call she speedily rallies."

1280. a.k.a. Glen Ellen.

1281. Four feet by four feet by eight feet.

1282. Canaan.

1283. Universitas Viridis Montis.

1284. It is comprised of the counties of Orleans, Essex, and Caledonia.

1285. The place where the world's largest scarecrow was built.

1286. Author of the *Vermont Historical Gazetteer*.

1287. Jerry Greenfield and Bennett Cohen.

1288. The new one has a tree and now Vermont is on top.

1289. Ethan Allen's second wife.

Final Jeopardy

1290. The birthplace of Vermont.

Answers:
The Category Is Vermont

Single Jeopardy

1258. What is milk?
1259. What is Act 250? (Or what is the Land Capability and Development Act?)
1260. What is the name of our state's professional minor league baseball club?
1261. What do we call pouring hot maple syrup on snow? (Usually served with pickles and doughnuts.)
1262. What is the state insect?
1263. What is the start of deer season with firearms?
1264. What is the Morgan?
1265. What is the name of Lake Champlain's answer to the Loch Ness Monster?
1266. What is the telephone area code for the entire state of Vermont?
1267. What is the state bird?
1268. What is "Across the Fence"?
1269. What did the Yorkers call the Green Mountain Boys?
1270. What is Barre known as?
1271. What is "Mud Season"?
1272. What is located in Barre?

Double Jeopardy

1273. What does Vergennes claim to be?
1274. What is fancy?
1275. What is the name of a ski area in Woodstock?
1276. What is the inscription on Robert Frost's gravesite?
1277. What is the device used to determine the thickness of maple syrup?
1278. What are towns in Windham County?
1279. What is one verse of "Hail, Vermont," the state song?
1280. What is Sugarbush North?
1281. What are the dimensions of a cord of wood?
1282. What is the northernmost, easternmost town in Vermont?
1283. What is the Latin for University of the Green Mountains from which the shorthand UVM was formed?
1284. What is the Northeast Kingdom?
1285. What is St. Albans? (Also credited with the world's largest ice cream sundae, pancake, and snowman.)
1286. Who was Abby Maria Hemenway?
1287. Who are the founders of Ben & Jerry's Ice Cream?

1288. What is the new Vermont license plate?

1289. Who was Fanny Montresor Buchanan Allen?

Final Jeopardy

1290. What is Windsor called? (Where in 1777 Vermont was declared an independent republic.)

1291.

What is the Vermont Raptor Center?

a. A discussion center for troubled Vermont teenagers.
b. The headquarters of the Green Mountain Club's Sunset Committee.
c. A rehabilitation center for impaired birds of prey.
d. The Center for Rehabilitated Addicts Promoting Teenage Organized Recreation.

Answer

c. A rehabilitation center for impaired birds of prey (owls, hawks, and eagles are all raptors) operated by the Vermont Institute of Natural Science. Color it good.

CHAPTER 22

Sea Shell City
and Other Vermont Landmarks

In Vermont most anything can be a landmark. We even passed landmark legislation (the billboard law) so we could see them better. People are landmarks. Stores are landmarks. Farms are landmarks. It's easier to proclaim things like these landmarks in Vermont since people and stores and farms tend to stay put longer here. Below are .000076% of Vermont's landmarks with our apologies to the others we (of course) considered but left out.

Match the landmark to the town:

_____ 1292.	Joe's Pond	a. Alburg
_____ 1293.	The Old Stone House	b. Brandon
_____ 1294.	Sea Shell City	c. Brownington
_____ 1295.	The Alburg Auction Barn	d. Cabot and Danville
_____ 1296.	Eureka Schoolhouse (oldest in Vermont)	e. Charlotte
		f. Danby
_____ 1297.	Vermont Wildflower Farm	g. Essex Junction
_____ 1298.	Hyde Log Cabin (oldest log cabin)	h. Ferrisburg
		i. Grand Isle
_____ 1299.	Green Mountain Audubon Nature Center	j. Huntington
		k. Middlesex
_____ 1300.	Button Bay State Park	l. Morrisville
_____ 1301.	The Vermont Country Store	m. Pittsford
_____ 1302.	The Morgan Horse Farm	n. St. George
_____ 1303.	The Discovery Museum	o. Springfield
_____ 1304.	Polka Dot Diner	p. Weston and Rockingham
_____ 1305.	Wrightsville Dam	q. Weybridge
_____ 1306.	Rocky Ridge Golf Course	r. White River Junction

The answers to Chapter 22 begin on page 221.

_____ 1307. New England Maple
Museum

_____ 1308. Cadys Falls Commission
Sales

_____ 1309. The Peel Gallery of
Fine Art

Name the town where the following landmarks are located:

1310. The Stone Village _____

1311. Smugglers' Notch _____

1312. Thunder Road Speedway _____

1313. Pavilion Office Building _____

1314. The *Ticonderoga* _____

1315. Rock of Ages Quarry _____

1316. Santa's Land _____

1317. The Scott Covered Bridge over the
West River _____

1318. The Floating Bridge _____

1319. Identify the statue on the Capitol dome in Montpelier.

    a. A cow
    b. Thomas Chittenden
    c. The Goddess of Agriculture
    d. Ethan Allen

1320. Whose statue is on the portico of the state house?

    a. Ethan Allen
    b. Thomas Chittenden
    c. George Washington
    d. Seth Warner

1321. The Bennington Battle Monument commemorates a battle fought
in

    a. Bennington, Vermont.
    b. Bennington, New York.
    c. Hoosick Falls, New York.
    d. Manchester, Vermont.

1322. Where would you be apt to find the *Spirit of Ethan Allen*?

1323. The Daniel Webster Monument is located in

   a. Stratton.
   b. Arlington.
   c. Wilmington.
   d. Maine.

1324. The Norman Rockwell Exhibit is located in

   a. Burlington.
   b. Manchester.
   c. Arlington.
   d. Rutland.

1325. When driving into Bristol from the east (traveling south on Route 116) you can't miss* a large boulder, flat on one side, with _____ printed on it.

   a. a quote from Ethan Allen
   b. the Lord's Prayer
   c. a poem from Robert Frost
   d. "Welcome to Bristol"

1326. Dedicated in 1890 by Franklin Fairbanks and containing a planetarium, nineteenth century treasures and three thousand stuffed animals, among other exhibits, the Fairbanks Museum is found in

   a. Brattleboro.
   b. White River Junction.
   c. Winooski.
   d. St. Johnsbury.

1327. St. Albans displays a monument commemorating a victory over a

   a. bobcat.
   b. flood.
   c. wolf.
   d. thief.

1328. What is the tallest man-made structure in the state of Vermont?

1329. In Sharon there is a monument and museum, open year-round, memorializing the birthplace of the founder of one of America's important religions, the _____.

*Actually, it's so near the road that the statement might be taken literally.

1330. When the Vermont State Prison closed in 1975, it was the country's oldest prison (built in 1808). Now it has become

   a. a school.
   b. an apartment building.
   c. a rehabilitation center.
   d. a museum.

1331. The town of Proctor contains an unusual sight. What is it?

   a. A fort
   b. A volcano
   c. A castle
   d. Cable cars

1332. The Catholic church in Waitsfield on Route 100 is called

   a. Our Lady of the Purple Bathtub
   b. Our Lady of the Snows
   c. Our Lady of the Mountains
   d. Our Lady of the Mogul *

1333. What is Fort Independence in Orwell named for?

   a. Vermont Independence Day
   b. The U.S. Declaration of Independence
   c. The capture of Fort Ticonderoga
   d. Washington's victory at Yorktown

1334. A prominent display in the Smithsonian Museum of Natural History in Washington, D.C., depicts

   a. gathering maple syrup in Derby.
   b. workers in the granite quarries at Barre.
   c. skiers on a Vermont ski slope.
   d. hikers on Mt. Mansfield.

1335. Danville is the headquarters for the American Society of

   a. Stone Cutters.
   b. Antique Dealers.
   c. the Historical Registry.
   d. Dowsers.

*One of the editors spent eight years in a Catholic grammar school, and the other was raised (through eight years) a Congregationalist before the family converted to Catholicism. One went to St. Michael's College, the other to Trinity. We both (attempt to) practice the faith—so we figure we're allowed a little fun since it's at our own expense.

1336. Sand Bar State Park is located in

    a. Milton.
    b. South Hero.
    c. Colchester.
    d. Isle La Motte.

1337. Frederick Law Olmstead, who designed Shelburne Farms, also designed what famous spot in New York City?

1338. In Derby, Vermont, there is something strange about the home of one of the residents. What is it?

    a. It floats.
    b. It is built in a tree.
    c. The U.S.–Canadian border runs through it.
    d. It's haunted.

1339. Where is the Justin Morrill homestead?

1340. St. Johnsbury has the oldest unaltered _____ in the United States.

    a. diner
    b. museum
    c. art gallery
    d. library

1341. Why is the sixteen-sided church in Richmond sixteen-sided?

1342. One of the most interesting grave sites in Vermont is in the Middlebury Cemetery. Resting there is

    a. Ethan Allen.
    b. the remains of Sergeant Preston's dog, King.
    c. an Egyptian mummy.
    d. an Eskimo daddy.

Match the following with the town:

_____	1343. The library built on a bridge	a. Calais
_____	1344. Stephen A. Douglas's birthplace	b. Woodford
_____	1345. Justin Morgan's burial place	c. Lyndonville
_____	1346. Vermont's smallest covered bridge	d. Whitingham
_____	1347. Highest village in the state	e. Randolph
_____	1348. Birthplace of Brigham Young	f. Brandon

218

1349. The Bennington Monument is made of

    a. New York dolomite.
    b. Vermont marble.
    c. Vermont granite.
    d. Georgia marble.

1350. It was created by Walter Hendricks. Robert Frost was an original trustee. Built on Potash Hill, it opened in 1948. It is?

    a. The Bread Loaf Writers' Conference Complex
    b. Marlboro College
    c. Goddard College
    d. The Dorset Playhouse

Questions about the Pictures

(Left) This landmark is beside what is perhaps Vermont's most imposing landmark, which is (1351.) _____.

(Right) This is the (1352.) _____ Tower in the city of (1353.) _____.

This beautiful building is the Windham County (1354.)
_____ in the town of (1355.) _____.

This structure houses the Vermont Historical Society. It is called the
(1356.) _____ Building.

Answers:
Sea Shell City and Other Vermont Landmarks

1292. d. Cabot and Danville
1293. c. Brownington. (Built by Reverend Alexander Lucius Twilight, the first black in America to receive a college degree.)
1294. b. Brandon
1295. a. Alburg. (We figured you'd get this one.)
1296. o. Springfield
1297. e. Charlotte
1298. i. Grand Isle
1299. j. Huntington
1300. h. Ferrisburg
1301. p. Weston and Rockingham
1302. q. Weybridge
1303. g. Essex Junction
1304. r. White River Junction (a village in Hartford)
1305. k. Middlesex
1306. n. St. George
1307. m. Pittsford
1308. l. Morrisville
1309. f. Danby
1310. Chester
1311. Cambridge (Stowe and Jeffersonville were good guesses!)
1312. Barre
1313. Montpelier
1314. Shelburne (specifically, the Shelburne Museum).
1315. Barre (more technically, Graniteville).
1316. Putney
1317. Townshend
1318. Brookfield. (The bridge is 294 feet long, and floats on 380 polystyrene floats. It originally floated on barrels.)
1319. c. Ceres, the Goddess of Agriculture, holding sheaves of wheat. It is carved from white pine from the state of—sorry—Washington.
1320. a. Ethan Allen
1321. c. Hoosick Falls, New York (originally the town of Wallomsack). General Stark decided to surprise the British five miles from the supply depot at Bennington.
1322. On Lake Champlain. The *Spirit of Ethan Allen* is a replica of a vintage stern-wheeler which offers scenic rides and dinner cruises.
1323. a. Stratton.

1324. c. Arlington, where Rockwell lived and worked for many years. Many of his subjects for *Saturday Evening Post* covers were Arlington residents.

1325. b. the Lord's Prayer. It was commissioned in 1891 by Joseph Greene, who was thankful for reaching that point safely while hauling logs.

1326. d. St. Johnsbury.

1327. c. wolf. We got the following from *Sketches of Early Life in St. Albans, Vermont*:

> A ferocious wolf that had been ravaging the northeastern part of Franklin county was now hiding on Aldis hill. Sheep, calves, and swine had been killed. . . . [Townspeople said] 'Call Lawrence Brainerd. He will get the wolf!' He was a man of powerful physique, great sagacity, undaunted courage, and an expert marksman . . . [Brainerd and his sons] climbed the hill where men and horses were running around in aimless confusion . . . a great shaggy head protruded from a crevice in the rock (at the highest point of the ledge). . . . When the wolf was fairly out of cover, Mr. Brainerd fired, and the great beast made one plunge forward, struck his head to the ground and lay dead with a bullet in his heart.

1328. The Bennington Battle Monument, which stands 306 feet 4½ inches tall.

1329. Mormon religion. (Joseph Smith was born in Sharon.)

1330. b. an apartment building.

1331. c. The Wilson Castle, a mid-nineteenth century castle.

1332. b. Our Lady of the Snows

1333. a. Vermont Independence Day

1334. b. workers in the granite quarries at Barre.

1335. d. Dowsers (people who search for water with a divining rod).

1336. a. Milton.

1337. Central Park

1338. c. The U.S.–Canadian border runs through it.

1339. Strafford. Sen. Justin Morrill served in Congress for nearly forty-four years. As author of the Land Grants Act of 1862, which gave public lands to the agricultural colleges of each state, he is probably the Vermonter with the most buildings named after him in the U.S.

1340. c. art gallery. (It was built in 1873.)

1341. There is one side for each man that built it plus the belfry for one man. The seventeen men represented five denominations. And from *School Bells Among Green Hills*, a fascinating and valuable edition on education in Vermont by the Vermont Association of Retired Teachers (Essex Publishing Company: Essex Junction,

Vermont, 1975), comes this: "In Brookline is the country's only round schoolhouse. It was built in 1822 by a Dr. Wilson, who was actually an infamous highwayman from England, known to his European companions as Thunderbolt. Fearing that the authorities would some day discover his identity, he built his brick schoolhouse in the round so that, from any part of the schoolroom, he could keep an eye out for approaching danger."

1342. c. an Egyptian mummy
1343. c. Lyndonville
1344. f. Brandon
1345. e. Randolph
1346. a. Kent's Corner in Calais
1347. b. Woodford
1348. d. Whitingham
1349. a. New York dolomite.
1350. b. Marlboro College
1351. the Bennington Monument
1352. Ethan Allen
1353. Burlington
1354. Courthouse
1355. Newfane
1356. Pavilion

1357.

Who was Clarina Howard Nichols?

Answer

Clarina Howard Nichols of West Townshend was a fierce battler for women's rights in Vermont 150 years ago. She wrote and then edited the Windham County *Democrat* of Brattleboro. Step by tedious step she labored to secure rights for women from a legislature comprised solely of men, elected solely by men. The picture of this woman riding a stage in the mud and dust to Montpelier before there were electric lights, before there was a state of California, before there was a Civil War, to cross swords on the same ideological battlefield that exists today (even as this book goes to print) provides a perspective on the times that is truly priceless.

The process that Nichols began has continued year by year, decade by decade, even transcending centuries themselves as one by one women's rights were secured. And they were such nitty-gritty rights too: the right to inherit and bequeath property, the right to insure the life of their husbands for their sole use (to be beneficiary), the right to vote in school district meetings (1880), the right to vote (1919), and the right to serve on juries (1943). We should applaud (with gusto) those still fighting for women's rights on *both* sides of the contemporary issue of whether or not Vermont needs an ERA. But a pause, please, for those thousands of ghosts that trod Vermont on the same pilgrimage when everyday life was so very much crueler and the political system was so very much less benign.

CHAPTER 23

"Vermont Is a Land I Love"*
Familiar Quotations—Yankee Style

In Vermont we are particularly aware of what people say about us. Perhaps that is because we share a unique heritage and live in a land that particularly bespeaks individualism. We have placed legal graffiti in the form of quotes about Vermont on the very walls of the state house. We delight in the notions (accurate and inaccurate) that outsiders have about us. Vermonters also have their own literature and their own history. From all this comes our own listing of familiar quotations. Let's see if you're conversant with it.

Fill in the following: (Hint: The spaces provided indicate the number of words in each.)

1358. "Home is a place that when you go there _____ _____ _____ _____ _____ _____." (Robert Frost)

1359. "Surrender in the name of the Great Jehova and _____ _____ _____." (Ethan Allen)

1360. "I do not choose to _____ _____ _____ _____ _____ _____ _____ _____." (Calvin Coolidge)

1361. "There is no more Yankee than Polynesian in me but when I go

*Calvin Coolidge said it in 1927. We all feel it.

The answers to Chapter 23 begin on page 230.

to Vermont I feel like I am _____ _____
_____ _____ _____." (Bernard DeVoto)

1362. "Something there is that doesn't _____ _____ _____."
(Robert Frost)

1363. "The gods of the hills are not _____ _____ _____
_____ _____." (Ethan Allen)

1364. "_____ _____ _____ _____ _____ and keep
the column well closed up." (Gen. John Sedgwick)

1365. "Vermonters will do nothing you tell them to; most anything that
you _____ _____ _____." (Calvin Coolidge)

1366. "You men of northern Vermont . . . living among its rocks and
mountains in a region which may be called the _____
of America—you are the people here who have had hearts full of
love of freedom which exists in mountain people and who have
the indomitable spirit and the unconquerable will which we
always associate with the lake and mountain lands." (Viscount
James Bryce)

Who said it?

a. George Dewey
b. Stephen Douglas
c. Ira Allen
d. Calvin Coolidge
e. Dick Snelling

f. Tom Salmon
g. George Aiken
h. Prince Otto von Bismarck
i. Sinclair Lewis

_____ 1367. "I love Vermont because of her hills and valleys, her
scenery and invigorating climate, but most of all, because
of her indomitable people."

_____ 1368. "The best way to kill something in Vermont is to man-
date it."

_____ 1369. "My idea of a republic is a little state in the north of your
great country . . . Vermont."

_____ 1370. "Vermont is *not* for sale."

_____ 1371. "You may fire when ready, Gridley."

_____ 1372. "Vermont is the most glorious spot on the face of the globe for a man to be born in, provided he emigrates when he is very young."

_____ 1373. "I know of no country that abounds in a greater diversity of hill and dale."

_____ 1374. "I like Vermont because it is quiet, because you have a population that is solid and not driven by the American mania—that mania which considers a town of 4,000 twice as good as a town of 2,000."

_____ 1375. "Either impeach him or get off his back."

Who said the following of whom?

1376. "I soon began to learn that, first of all, she wanted everything kept clean about her, that she wanted things done promptly and systematically and that at the bottom of everything she wanted absolute honesty and frankness."

    a. Lt. Gov. Peter Smith of Gov. Madeleine Kunin.
    b. Booker T. Washington of the Vermont schoolteacher that taught him to read.
    c. Calvin Coolidge of Mrs. Calvin Coolidge.
    d. Abraham Lincoln of his Vermont-born housekeeper.

1377. "I am but one in fifty-five million; still in the opinion of this one fifty-five-millionth of the country's population, it would be hard to better President _____'s Administration."

    a. George Aiken about Herbert Hoover's administration.
    b. Mrs. Calvin Coolidge about Calvin Coolidge's administration.
    c. Mark Twain about Chester Arthur's administration.
    d. James Garfield about Chester Arthur's administration.

To whom did each refer?

1378. Walter Prescott Webb said the following of whom?
He "broke his health and brought himself to the grave prematurely by the intensity of his inactivity."

1379. George Washington said the following of whom?
"There is an original something in him that commands attention."

1380. Sen. Jacob Collamer, President Lincoln's confidant, said of a Vermont town, "The good people of _____ have less incentive than others to yearn for heaven." Of which Vermont town was he speaking?

Fill in the blanks:

"There are the Redcoats; they will be ours or tonight (1381.)
_____ sleeps a widow," said General (1382.) _____ *
before the Battle of (1383.) _____.

Who said the following:

"The New Hampshire Grants in particular, a country unpeopled and almost unknown in the last war, now abounds in the most active and most rebellious race on the continent and hangs like a gathering storm on my left."
(1384.) Gen. _____

1385. What did Ethan Allen say when he demanded the surrender of Fort Ticonderoga?

   a. "Surrender or I shall lay this fort as low as Sodom and Gomorrah."
   b. "My apologies for the disruption; may I have your sword, sir?"
   c. "Put on your pants and show us where you keep the rum."
   d. None of the above (as far as we know).

During the Vietnam War, a Vermont politician gave the president some advice on the war that received national attention and in fact was pretty much followed.

1386. The politician was _____.

1387. His advice was to _____

_____.

The most well-known song about Vermont is "Moonlight in Vermont." It even survived a rendition by popular country-and-western singer (1388.) _____. How well do you know the lyrics?

(1389.) _____ in a stream, falling leaves, a
(1390.) _____
Moonlight in Vermont

Icy finger waves, (1391.) _____ on a mountainside
(1392.) _____ light in Vermont

*He came from New Hampshire but it sure sounds like Vermont.

228

(1393.) _____ they sing down the
(1394.) _____ and travel each bend in the road

People who meet in this (1395.) _____ setting
Are so hypnotized by the lovely evening (1396.) _____
(1397.) _____

(1398.) _____ of a (1399.) _____, moonlight in
Vermont
You and I and moonlight in Vermont.

We, therefore, the inhabitants, on said tract of land, are at present without law or government, and may be truly said to be in a state of nature;
consequently a right remains to the people of said Grants to form a
government best suited to secure their (1400.)
_____, well being and (1401.) _____.

Vermont's Declaration of Independence
Westminster, January 15, 1777.

Answers:
"Vermont Is a Land I Love"

1358. " Home is a place that when you go there *they have to take you in.*"

1359. "Surrender in the name of the Great Jehova and *the Continental Congress.*"

1360. "I do not choose to *run for President in nineteen hundred and twenty-eight.*"

1361. "There is no more Yankee than Polynesian in me but when I go to Vermont I feel like I am *traveling towards my own place.*"

1362. "Something there is that doesn't *love a wall.*"

1363. "The gods of the hills are not *the gods of the valleys.*"

1364. *"Put the Vermonters in front* and keep the column well closed up." This command was issued at the Battle of Gettysburg. Also at the Battle of Gettysburg, General Doubleday, watching the Second Vermont Brigade, shouted "Glory to God, glory to God, see the Vermonters go at it." During the Civil War it was Dixie's Gen. Stonewall Jackson who was credited with the swiftest marches and greatest endurance. But the Vermonters proved his equal. The First Vermont marched thirty-two miles in a night and a day to reach Gettysburg on July 2nd. The Second Vermont Brigade marched 132 miles in six days in sweltry southern July heat to reach the battle July 1st.

1365. "Vermonters will do nothing you tell them to; most anything that you *ask them to.*"

1366. *Switzerland*

1367. d. Calvin Coolidge

1368. e. Dick Snelling

1369. h. Prince Otto Von Bismarck

1370. f. Tom Salmon

1371. a. George Dewey

1372. b. Stephen Douglas. In one of the great quirks of U.S. electoral history, Stephen Douglas, a native Vermonter, was defeated four to one in Vermont when he ran for president against a flatlander from Illinois named Abe Lincoln. Vermonters, it seemed, were more interested in issues like slavery than birth-right. (It may have helped, of course, that Lincoln was a Republican.)

1373. c. Ira Allen

1374. i. Sinclair Lewis

1375. g. George Aiken (referring to Richard Nixon).

1376. b. Booker T. Washington of his teacher Viola Knapp Ruffner.

1377. c. Mark Twain about President Arthur. Garfield might have said it but if he did it wasn't to anyone on the planet since the reason Arthur was president was because Garfield had been shot dead.

1378. Calvin Coolidge

1379. Ethan Allen

1380. Woodstock

1381. Molly Stark

1382. John Stark. (Earle Newton quotes Stark a hair differently, "There stand the Redcoats, today they are ours, or Molly Stark sleeps this night a widow.")

1383. Bennington

1384. John Burgoyne

1385. d. But we do know they did consume most of the fort's rum. Historian B.A. Botkin writes that one Israel Harris, who was present, passed on to his ancestors what he believed to be Ethan Allen's real words: "Come out of there, you goddam old rat." Most people like to believe he really did say "Surrender in the name of the Great Jehovah and the Continental Congress." (See question 1359.)

1386. George Aiken

1387. "Declare victory and leave." Judson Hale says this about the Aiken quote: "It's somehow comforting to Americans when a Vermonter acts like 'a Vermonter.' We all smiled and felt good inside when Aiken advised President Lyndon Johnson to declare the Vietnam War won and pull out the troops. It would not have been as amusing or even as wise if someone from another state had said it."

1388. Willie Nelson

1389. Pennies

1390. sycamore

1391. ski trails

1392. Snow

1393. Telegraph cables

1394. highway

1395. romantic

1396. summer

1397. breeze

1398. Warbling

1399. meadowlark

1400. property

1401. happiness

THE "HOW MANY" PAGE

From the list of numbers below, select the answers to the following questions. Use each listed number once.

2	4	20
2	5	30
3	14	36
3	16	75
3	17	175
4	18	246
4		

As of the summer of 1986, how many

_____ 1402. children does Madeleine Kunin have?

_____ 1403. state-wide elections (total) had Jim Jeffords, Dick Snelling, and Phil Hoff lost?

_____ 1404. ferry crossings are on Lake Champlain?

_____ 1405. dollars will register your car?

_____ 1406. state flags has Vermont had?

_____ 1407. covered bridges cross the Connecticut River?

_____ 1408. "organized" cities and towns does Vermont have?

_____ 1409. airports/airstrips are in Vermont?

_____ 1410. questions are on the written part of the state driver's exam?

_____ 1411. days does the regular deer season last?

_____ 1412. hospitals are there in Vermont?

_____ 1413. ski areas does Vermont have (not counting cross-country ski centers)?

_____ 1414. model airplanes are hanging in the lobby of Burlington International Airport?

_____ 1415. counties are there in Vermont?

_____ 1416. different people have served as Governor?

The answers to this section begin on page 234.

_____ 1417. days (minimum) must a Vermont public high school be in session each year?

_____ 1418. justices on the Vermont Supreme Court?

_____ 1419. State Houses has Vermont had?

_____ 1420. quarts in a gallon of Vermont maple syrup?

Answers:
The "How Many" Page

1402. 4 (1 daughter and 3 sons).
1403. 3
1404. 4 (Fort Ticonderoga, Grand Isle, Burlington, Charlotte).
1405. 36
1406. 3. (The first state flag was authorized in 1803. It was changed in 1821. The present flag was confirmed by law in 1862.)
1407. 2
1408. 246
1409. 18. Locations are South Burlington, Berlin, Clarendon, Bennington, Bondville, Dover, Fair Haven, Highgate, Island Pond, Lyndonville, Middlebury, Morrisville, Newport, North Windham, Post Mills, Springfield, Vergennes, and Warren (based on the Development and Community Affairs Agency's *Doing Business in Vermont*).
1410. 20. (16 must be answered correctly to pass the test.)
1411. 16
1412. 17. Brattleboro, Central Vermont, Copley, Fanny Allen, Gifford, Grace Cottage, Medical Center Hospital of Vermont, Mt. Ascutney, North Country, Northeastern Regional, Northwest, Porter, Rockingham, Rutland, Southwestern (formerly Putnam), Springfield, and the Veteran's Administration Hospital.
1413. 30 according to the 1984–85 Ski Vermont Winter Guide.
1414. 2 as we go to print, but the airport is being remodeled.
1415. 14. Addison, Bennington, Caledonia, Chittenden, Essex, Franklin, Grand Isle, Lamoille, Orange, Orleans, Rutland, Washington, Windham, and Windsor.
1416. 75
1417. 175 is the minimum mandated by the state.
1418. 5
1419. 3. The first one was built in 1808 and torn down in 1836. The second one was completed in 1838 and destroyed by fire in 1857. The present state house was dedicated in 1859.
1420. Even Yankees consider 4 quarts to be a gallon.

CHAPTER 24

Those That Labor in the Earth

"Those that labor in the earth," said Thomas Jefferson, "are the chosen people of God." Vermonters know that's an exaggeration—of sorts. Vermont without farmers could be a good place too but it could never be Vermont; and while there are lots of good places, there is only one Vermont. Ever since Vermont began, those that worked the land have defined our every contour—the economy, the politics, the villages and towns, indeed the very landscape that enwraps our lives. We know them by their sounds and sights and smells—the distant "chomp and grind" of a baler on a quiet June afternoon, a herd of cattle asteam in a barnyard yellow with the cold sun of January, the smell of fresh manure and new cut hay: signs of life and rebirth of labor and accomplishment. The chosen people of God? Maybe not. But close. Very close.

1421. On average what kind of cow is the largest at maturity?

    a. Holstein
    b. Jersey
    c. Guernsey
    d. Hereford

1422. During which of the following decades did Vermont lose the greatest number of farms?

    a. 1900–1910
    b. 1940–1950
    c. 1970–1980

The answers to Chapter 24 begin on page 245.

1423. Which kind of cow is the most popular among Vermont's farmers?

a. Holstein
b. Jersey
c. Guernsey
d. Ayrshire

1424. Vermont produces fewer pounds of milk per day now than it did in 1950.

a. True
b. False

1425. The average dairy cow in Vermont produces about how many quarts of milk a day?

a. 10
b. 25
c. 70
d. 110

1426. How many farms were there in Vermont according to the 1982 U.S. Census of Agriculture?

a. 517
b. 2,480
c. 6,315
d. 10,670

1427. What is the record price for a dairy cow sold in Vermont?

a. $3,000
b. $30,000
c. $250,000
d. $1,300,000

1428. You are talking to two Vermonters, one from, say, Bridport and the other from, say, Norwich. In answer to the question, "Where do Vermonters milk their cows?" one says, "in the 'bahn'," the other says, "in the 'barrn.' " Which one says "bahn"?

a. The one from Bridport
b. The one from Norwich

1429. Vermont is number one in New England in total milk production.

a. True
b. False

1430. What percentage of Vermont farmers actually reside on their farms?

a. 65%
b. 85%
c. 95%
d. 100%

1431. Vermont is America's largest producer of maple syrup.

a. True
b. False

1432. In one year, Vermont farmers induce Vermont cows to produce

a. over 2 million pounds of milk.
b. over 200 million pounds of milk.
c. over 2 billion pounds of milk.

1433. In 1840 there were 291,948 people in Vermont. How many sheep were there?

a. 108,766
b. 291,948
c. 552,900
d. 1,681,814

1434. Based on the value of all dairy products sold in 1982, Vermont ranked _____ in the country.

a. 1st
b. 5th
c. 13th
d. 48th

1435. Something is perched on top of the V in the Vermont Seal of Quality label. What is it?

a. A cow
b. An apple
c. A cow eating an apple
d. A red clover

1436. In no other state does dairy account for as high a percentage of farm income as in Vermont.

   a. True
   b. False

The top three dairy producing counties in New England are found in Vermont. Name them.

1437. _____, 1438. _____, and 1439. _____.

1440. In 1984 the Vermont Department of Agriculture reported that the number of dairy farms in the state was decreasing.

   a. True
   b. False

1441. In 1984 Vermont chickens produced enough eggs to provide one a day for everyone in the state.

   a. True
   b. False

1442. About what percentage of Vermont's land area is being actively farmed?

   a. 5%
   b. 19%
   c. 31%
   d. 54%

1443. Vermont's highest apple-producing county is

   a. Grand Isle.
   b. Addison.
   c. Bennington.
   d. Windham.

1444. Vermont is losing farm land at about the rate of _____ acres a year.

   a. 13,000
   b. 30,000
   c. 52,000

Match the number with the kind of production in 1984 in Vermont:

_____ 1445. Number of honey bee colonies	a. 6,800
_____ 1446. Number of bushels of apples	b. 10,000
_____ 1447. Number of hogs and pigs	c. 14,000
_____ 1448. Number of sheep and lambs	d. 976,000
_____ 1449. Number of tons of corn silage	e. 1,212,312

Agri-ID's

Identify each of the following:

1450. The Bay State Cow Path

The "Bay State Cow Path," from Middlebury to Brattleboro, covered much of what is now Route 30. It was a route followed by Boston buyers wanting fresh meat for the Boston market.

1451. PTO

With apologies to parents and teachers, PTO also stands for Power Take Off, a device that radically changed the character of mechanized farm work in Vermont. "Hooking it up to the PTO" saved an awful lot of work. Located at the rear of a tractor, it allows the farmer to run machinery (often hauled behind the tractor) with power from the tractor itself—power that operates mowers, rakes, and so on. Running the baler off the PTO is much easier than off an engine perched on the baler (or what have you) itself.

1452. Rowen

Rowen is the second cutting of hay from a field. Since it grows slower than the "first cutting," it gathers more protein. Rowen is therefore more highly valued as feed. We like the description Richard Ketchum (of Blair and Ketchum's _Country Journal_) uses in the introduction to his (highly recommended) book of essays, _Second Cutting_: "You can't expect the same quantity the second time around, but you have a shot at putting up hay that is more tender and nutritious, with a high protein content and quality that won't deteriorate during the winter."

1453. Bag Balm

This ointment, made in Lyndonville, Vermont, is used for cows' udders. However, its soothing properties were discovered to be useful for humans too, and it soon became a standard item on the shelf above the sink where the milking machines are washed. It is applied to almost anything that hurts, chafes, or itches in and around the barn.

1454. A Sulky Plow

A plow that you sit on behind the horses rather than walk behind (a walking plow). For those interested, the Billings Farm Museum in Woodstock will hold its second plowing contest for oxen and horses in 1987. We found the event this year to be great and next year should be even better. One of these days we might even have our own team there.

1455. Docking

This is the process of cutting off a lamb's tail soon after birth. Although many methods have been used historically, one common technique today is to place a small rubber band around the tail until it works its way through and severs the tail completely. It takes about two weeks. Why cut off the tail? It hangs down from the wrong end of a sheep and soon becomes clogged with a substance that is not, unfortunately, as "white as snow." Sorry, Mary, but the tail comes off.

1456. RO Machine

A machine used in sugaring that has revolutionized (along with plastic tubing) the work process. It pumps sap up against a semi-permeable membrane at about 5000 pounds of pressure per square inch. Only pure water gets through. The remaining sap is 70–80% free of water. If you've ever boiled, you know what that means!

1457. "Canadian Chunk"

Penny Battison of Middlebury, a chronicler of horses and horse racing, describes one this way:
"'I beg your pardon, Canadian *what?*'
'Canadian Chunk'
It's Vermontese for the Canadian Horse, an old, somewhat obscure, but once highly desirable breed of draft horse with origins dating back to the 1600's."

1458. Pitman Rod

The shaft that drives a cutter bar of an old-style mowing machine. When they were made of wood, they often broke, becoming the source of many innovative blasphemies in the Vermont hills.

1459. Ferguson Hitch

A method of hitching farm equipment drawn behind a tractor under the *front* wheels and not the back wheels. This method helps alleviate one of the most dangerous of farm mishaps. If, for instance, a plow gets hung up, the back wheels of a tractor keep turning and the front of the tractor rears up. With the Ferguson hitch, the force of the tractor pulling when it can't go forward is transferred to the front wheels, holding them down on the ground.

1460. Heifer

A young cow that has not given birth and therefore has yet to produce income for the farmer.

1461. PDM

Short for Predicted Difference in Milk. This is a figure that tells the farmer how much more milk he can expect to get from cows produced by a bull's sperm *above* the average bull's daughter. In other words, the records of the thousands of daughters of any one bull are kept, compared to the daughters of other bulls, and reported to prospective buyers of the sperm. Farming is high tech, folks, and that's no bull.

1462. The Extension Service and Agricultural Experiment Station at the University of Vermont provides which publications free of charge to the general public?

    a. "Is Manure Odor Bothering You?"
    b. "Semen Handling on the Farm"
    c. "Teat Dipping Facts"
    d. All of the above

1463. The Brown Swiss is a breed of

    a. goat.
    b. sheep.
    c. cow.
    d. goose.

1464. Which breed of cattle are used for oxen?

    a. Holstein
    b. Ayrshires
    c. Charolais
    d. All of the above

1465. When ordering horses and oxen around, you often hear the words "gee" and "haw."* One means left and one means right. Which is which?

*Actually you are apt to hear a lot of other words as well but they are more easily understood and this is a family book.

1466. Which kind of cow gives milk with the higher butterfat content, Holsteins or Jerseys?

The Vermont Farm Show is held in (1467.) _____ (town) in (1468.) _____ (month).

1469. How did Ben Mason, Director of the Shelburne Museum, transport a 7½ ton silo from Passumpsic to Shelburne?

    a. By open-bed truck
    b. By train
    c. By helicopter
    d. By horse-drawn wagons

When you wonder if your neighbor's pig has had her young yet, you ask: Has she *pigged*? What about

1470.   rabbits?   _____

1471.   sheep?   _____

1472.   cows?   _____

1473.   goats?   _____

1474. What is inside the giant worm Ben Cole is playing with in his dad's barnyard in South Newbury?

1475. According to a study at the University of Vermont, Connecticut dairy farmers paid an average of $18.67 "per cow" in taxes in 1985, while Vermont's dairy farmers paid an average of

a. $15.30.
b. $29.60.
c. $51.10.

1476. On September 26, 1908, Edward Moote of Weathersfield accomplished a tremendous feat. He

a. milked 32 cows in an hour.
b. cut, split, and piled 5 cord of 4-foot wood in a day.
c. with his team of Durhams, he plowed 32 acres in a day.
d. debeaked 4,200 chickens in a day.

1477. Vermont farmers produce about _____ of New England's milk.

a. 10%
b. 40%
c. 70%

1478. What do the following people have in common: Peter Genier, Ned Dunbar, Mike Palmer, Ed Hazen, Bill Radar, and Paul Chateauvert?

a. They all milk goats.
b. They all produce honey.
c. They all keep Jersey cows.
d. They all raise rabbits for meat.

The Maple Corner

1479. How many years does it take to grow a tree big enough to tap?

a. 20
b. 40

1480. How many gallons of sap does it take to make a gallon of maple syrup?

1481. What is the minimum size a tree should be before it's tapped?

a. 6 inches in diameter
b. 10 inches in diameter
c. 15 inches in diameter

1482. In the 1980's Vermont has out-produced its closest competitor (New York) in syrup production by about _____.

    a. 10%

    b. 50%

    c. 100%

1483. A tree 22 inches in diameter will support 3 taps.

    a. True

    b. False

1484. Vermont's leading county in maple syrup production is

    a. Bennington.

    b. Franklin.

    c. Windsor.

    d. Caledonia.

1485. Identify: Noel Perrin

Answers:
Those That Labor in the Earth

1421. a. Holstein
1422. b. 1940–1950. In this decade we lost 4,539 farms, more than one a day.
1423. a. Holstein
1424. b. False
1425. b. 25. While many will think this low, the number was estimated by using 12,500 pounds of milk per year per cow as the basis quantity for all breeds in a 9-month lactation, and by estimating a quart of milk to weigh 2 pounds. We know, for instance, a good little family farm on the Connecticut River where about 50 Holsteins average 32 quarts a day.
1426. c. 6,315 farms. As of January 1, 1985, there were 3,113 dairy farms.
1427. d. The most expensive cow sold in the U.S. was sold at the Lylehaven Farm in East Montpelier on July 13, 1985. She went for $1.3 million. "Mist" will have to produce 2,166,666 quarts to pay for herself at the store. If she milks for 10 years, 9 months a year, she will have to average 802 quarts a day, or 1,604 pounds, a figure very close to her weight. Let's hope her daughters are good ones.
1428. b. The one from Norwich
1429. a. True
1430. b. 85%
1431. a. True
1432. c. over 2 billion pounds of milk.
1433. d. 1,681,814 (about 6 per person).
1434. c. 13th
1435. d. A red clover
1436. a. True
1437.–1439. Addison, Franklin, Orleans
1440. a. True. By about 60 a year.
1441. b. False. Not even close. They'd have to produce about three times as many as the 5,416,000 dozen they did lay.
1442. b. 19%. In 1920 it was 73%. Think about that. We're only talking 66 years.
1443. b. Addison.
1444. a. 13,000 acres. Another, more recent study puts it at between 17,000 and 20,000 acres.
1445. b. 10,000 honey bee colonies

1446. d. 976,000 bushels of apples

1447. a. 6,800 hogs and pigs

1448. c. 14,000 sheep and lambs

1449. e. 1,212,312 tons (as in 2,000 pounds each!) of silage

1450.–1461. Agri-ID's: Answers are with the questions.

1462. d. All of the above. After the first three publications you have to pay 15 cents apiece. But these three are free.

1463. c. cow

1464. d. all of the above

1465. "Gee" is right and "haw" is left.

1466. Jerseys. Jersey owners refer to Holstein milk as "chalk and water." Holstein owners seldom dispute this but claim they have forgotten the insult by the time they reach the bank.

1467. Barre

1468. January

1469. c. By helicopter

1470. kindled

1471. lambed

1472. calved

1473. kidded

1474. Silage. Instead of building silos, many Vermont farmers are blowing their hay and corn silage into large plastic bags.

1475. c. $51.10, highest of the five states in the Northeast studied.

1476. b. By 4:15 p.m., he was done. Moote (50 years old and 150 pounds) added another 1/8 of a cord for "good measure" and then, to the cheers of the crowd, he collected $100 for his task and was placed atop the pile for pictures. Over $5,000 in bets had been laid. Among the losers was the journalist Samuel G. Blythe. See what interesting things you can read about as a member of the Vermont Historical Society?

1477. b. 40%

1478. b. They all produce honey.

1479. b. 40

1480. 40

1481. b. 10" in diameter

1482. b. 50%

1483. a. True

1484. b. Franklin.

1485. Vermont's first, second, and third person "rural," he's also written a book on amateur maple sugaring.

1486.

What was the Bolton War?

Answer

The Bolton War was a labor dispute in 1846 involving Irish railroad laborers on the Vermont Central Railroad. Historian T.D. Seymour Bassett* calls it "probably the first major work stoppage in Vermont history." A hostage was taken and the laborers holed up in Jones's Hotel in Jonesville.

Bassett reports the rest as follows in the Summer 1981 issue of *Vermont History*: "On the eve of Fourth of July, the sheriff, needing reinforcements, called for the Burlington Light Infantry. The infantry mustered and marched in a holiday spirit, under Joseph Hatch, wholesale grocer. A fire company received muskets and joined the army to remove this rebellious Irish obstacle to American progress and prosperity. Faced with such a bristling array of Yankee force and persuaded by a Roman Catholic priest, the men released Barker [the hostage] and dispersed without violence. The authorities jailed a dozen in Burlington, and a good many never received their earnings."

*As an eighteen-year-old freshman at St. Michael's College in the spring of 1960, one of the editors was writing a paper on the Haldimand Negotiations using the specialized resources at UVM. Needing assistance he asked it of a busy gentleman working there. With patience and enthusiasm, this UVM professor encouraged and, without intrusion, gave direction to sources along with a helpful hint or two on the thesis itself. Years passed before this teenager realized it was Professor Bassett. He never forgot that day or the man who helped a young snotty-nosed Vermont kid from Newbury when he really didn't need to. Now *there* was a teacher.

CHAPTER 25

The Business of Vermont

It was a Vermonter, after all, who said that the business of America was business. For the most part, Vermont business follows the contours of the landscape—it's small and fashioned to fit this "Yankee Kingdom" of ours. There is indeed a Vermont "business ethic" that reflects our dispositions on other matters as well; its hallmarks are frugality, a keen eye for the possible, and conservatism in matters financial. Now of course Vermont has become a land where "high-tech entrepreneurs" can have a go at it and breathe clean air at the same time. In a sense we have come full circle, for that is much of what Vermont was all about in the very beginning. And on balance, Vermont's human-scale environment has coexisted amicably with the profit motive. A twinkle in the eye has often accompanied the jingle of change in the pocket or the clink of the cash register. Anyone who has ever put together a high-school yearbook in a small Vermont town understands the deal struck when a local businessperson pays for "advertising" in the back. It's a gift, of course, and that fact is not lost on either party. The deal cut makes it more palatable for both. We like our businesspeople in Vermont. Perhaps that's because we've gotten to know them better here.

1487. Skyline Nursery in Springfield offers a unique service. They will

    a. move and replant your very large trees.
    b. harvest and can your garden.
    c. tap your sugar bush.
    d. plant your Christmas tree "farm."

The answers to Chapter 25 begin on page 258.

1488. Leader's in St. Albans and Grimm's in Rutland are the only manufacturers of these in the country. What do they make?

1489. Clint Fiske owns a bookstore in Cuttingsville. There is something different about it. What?

    a. It features only foreign language books.
    b. The books are absolutely free.
    c. It sells only books about Vermont or by Vermonters.
    d. It's haunted.

1490. What is Vermont's most valuable crop, estimated at a value of $275 million in 1985?

1491. David Moore, Inc., of North Pomfret is the only

    a. producer of artificial maple syrup in Vermont.
    b. mechanical-organ builder in Vermont.
    c. manufacturer of Vermont-made saddles.
    d. real estate dealer in Vermont specializing in property on the moon.

1492. Who is the largest manufacturer of cast-iron wood stoves in the world?

1493. The only Vermont firm ranking in the top 20 of *New England Business Monthly*'s list of New England's top 250 privately held companies was

    a. Pizzagalli Construction.
    b. C & S Wholesale Grocers.
    c. Ben and Jerry's Ice Cream.
    d. Cabot Farmer's Cooperative.

1494. In May of 1986, the unemployment rate in Vermont according to the Agency of Development and Community Affairs was

    a. 2.4%.
    b. 5.2%.
    c. 11.1%.

1495. Not including branch offices, how many banks are there in Vermont?

    a. 37
    b. 52
    c. 74

1496. In 1985 over 200,000 _____ were sold in Vermont, producing $16 million in revenue.

   a. cords of firewood
   b. season ski-lift tickets
   c. calves
   d. bicycles

1497. Michelle and David Holzapfel of "Applewoods" in Marlboro create unique sculptures out of

   a. apples.
   b. apple wood exclusively.
   c. roots of trees.
   d. granite.

1498. What is the WBOV? (It is not a radio station.)

1499. The first real production line in America was located at an arsenal in Windsor during the 1840's.

   a. True
   b. False

1500. How many manufacturers are there in Grand Isle County?

   a. 1
   b. 8
   c. 24
   d. 53

1501. For almost 4 decades the largest employer in Franklin County has been

   a. Green Mountain Printing and Publishing, Enosburg.
   b. Exon Industries, Sheldon Springs.
   c. Phillips Metallurgical, Swanton.
   d. Union Carbide, St. Albans.

1502. A famous Vermont trucking company is named after a town in the Northeast Kingdom. It is?

1503. One of Vermont's famous discount department stores is on the beautiful Barre–Montpelier Road. It has a man's name. What is it?

1504. The following people are all in the same Vermont business.

Dan Roberts, West Fairlee
Bucky Cole, North Pomfret
Bill Taber, Cuttingsville
Junior Comstock, East Corinth

What is it?

"Out-of-towners may call collect" is a phrase associated with Red (1505.)
_____, who is in the (1506.) _____ business.

1507. This program has loaned over a million dollars since 1978 to
Vermont entrepreneurs and has helped to launch 300 new small
businesses in Vermont. The name of the program is

a. Bootstraps Incorporated.
b. Job Start.
c. Green Mountain Entrepreneurs.
d. The Little Guy.

1508. When you hear the name "Chuck Perkins," you think of

a. Garden Way.
b. WCAX-TV.
c. Harrington Hams.
d. the Alpine Shop.

1509. The largest private employer in Vermont is _____.

Match the businessperson with the business:

_____ 1510. Valerie Chapman	a. IBM
_____ 1511. Elbert G. Moulton	b. Vermont Castings
_____ 1512. Ted Toole	c. Pompanoosuc Mills Corp.
_____ 1513. Dwight Sargent	d. Green Mountain Marble
_____ 1514. Ed Townsend	e. Thermax Corporation
_____ 1515. Richard Clayton	f. St. Albans Cooperative Creamery
_____ 1516. Ryle Dow	g. Brattleboro Development Credit Corporation
_____ 1517. Dick Chapman	h. United McGill

1518. What are SBDC's?

Place the business with the place in which it's located:

_____ 1519. H.K. Webster Co. (Blue
Seal Feeds)
_____ 1520. Idlenot Farm Dairy, Inc.
_____ 1521. International Business
Machines
_____ 1522. Simmonds Precision
_____ 1523. Ethan Allen, Inc.
(Furniture)
_____ 1524. Concord Manufacturing
Co. (Clothing)
_____ 1525. Lynda Lee Fashions, Inc.
_____ 1526. Bijur Lubricating Corp.
_____ 1527. The Book Press, Inc.
_____ 1528. Merrimaid Manufacturing, Inc.
(Underwear)
_____ 1529. Rock of Ages Corporation

a. Graniteville
b. Bennington
c. Essex Junction
d. Richford
e. Morrisville
f. Rutland
g. Brattleboro
h. Springfield
i. Vergennes
j. Orleans
k. Randolph

1530. Of the approximately 23,000 businesses listed in the *Vermont Business Phone Book and Manufacturers Directory*, how many are named "Ethan Allen"?

a. 18
b. 52
c. 230
d. 742

1531. How many are named "Green Mountain"?

a. 23
b. 170
c. 713
d. 1420

The Media Business

Match the daily newspaper with the town in which it is located:

_____ 1532. Barre-Montpelier
_____ 1533. Bennington
_____ 1534. Brattleboro
_____ 1535. Burlington
_____ 1536. Newport
_____ 1537. Rutland
_____ 1538. St. Albans
_____ 1539. St. Johnsbury

a. *Free Press*
b. *Caledonian-Record*
c. *Times-Argus*
d. *Banner*
e. *Messenger*
f. *Daily Herald*
g. *Reformer*
h. *Daily Express*

All told there are 67 local radio stations and weekly newspapers in Vermont. See if you can match the radio station and the paper that are located in the same place.

_____ 1540. *Addison County*   a. WCFR
                Independent   b. WJOY

_____ 1541. *White River Valley*   c. WCVR
                Herald   d. WFAD

_____ 1542. *Springfield Reporter*

_____ 1543. *Vanguard Press*

Business Associations

Match the person with the group with which they are associated:

_____ 1544. C. Harry Behney   a. Executive Director, GBIC
_____ 1545. Louise Magram Weiner   (Greater Burlington
_____ 1546. Peter A. Foote   Industrial Corporation)
_____ 1547. Patricia Heffernan   b. Executive Vice President,
                              Associated Industries of
                              Vermont
                   c. President, Women Business
                              Owners of Vermont
                   d. President, Vermont Retail
                              Association

1548. Roderick Stinehour has a business in Lunenburg, Vermont, deep in the Northeast Kingdom. What is it?

Business Districts

On the following pages are pictures of 6 Vermont business districts or "downtowns." Can you identify them?

_____ 1549. Rutland   _____ 1552. Montpelier
_____ 1550. Newport   _____ 1553. Burlington
_____ 1551. Brattleboro   _____ 1554. St. Johnsbury

Following these are 6 more. Identify them.

_____ 1555. Brandon   _____ 1558. Lyndonville
_____ 1556. Richford   _____ 1559. Orleans
_____ 1557. Middlebury   _____ 1560. Barton

A

B

C

254

D

E

F

255

A

B

C

D

E

F

257

Answers:
The Business of Vermont

1487. a. They will move and replant very large trees such as 50-foot trees with 16–17-inch diameters.
1488. Maple sugar evaporators. (However, they do have to compete heavily with manufacturers in Quebec.)
1489. d. It's haunted and is called the Haunted Mansion Bookstore.
1490. Marijuana. According to NORML (the National Organization for Reform of Marijuana Laws), Vermont ranks 25th in the nation in the production of marijuana.
1491. b. mechanical-organ builder in Vermont.
1492. Vermont Castings in Randolph
1493. b. C & S Wholesale Grocers of Brattleboro.
1494. b. 5.2%.
1495. a. 37. (And there are 66 credit unions.)
1496. a. cords of wood. (Another 300,000 cords were burned by the people who cut the wood.)
1497. c. roots of trees. They also use burls and butt logs with which they make sculptures, vases, and furniture.
1498. Women Business Owners of Vermont
1499. a. True
1500. a. 1—Phoenix Wire, Inc. They insulate the tiniest wires in the world with Teflon.
1501. d. Union Carbide employs about 400.
1502. St. Johnsbury Trucking
1503. Harry's
1504. Pulling and show cattle: they are all ox teamsters.
1505. Elmore
1506. construction
1507. b. Job Start.
1508. d. the Alpine Shop.
1509. IBM (International Business Machines)
1510. e. Thermax Corporation
1511. g. Brattleboro Development Credit Corporation
1512. d. Green Mountain Marble
1513. c. Pompanoosuc Mills Corporation
1514. h. United McGill
1515. b. Vermont Castings
1516. f. St. Albans Cooperative Creamery
1517. a. IBM

1518. Small Business Development Centers. They are operated by the UVM Extension Service.
1519. d. Richford
1520. h. Springfield
1521. c. Essex Junction
1522. i. Vergennes
1523. j. Orleans
1524. e. Morrisville
1525. f. Rutland
1526. b. Bennington
1527. g. Brattleboro
1528. k. Randolph
1529. a. Graniteville
1530. a. 18
1531. b. 170
1532. c. Barre–Montpelier *Times-Argus*
1533. d. Bennington *Banner*
1534. g. Brattleboro *Reformer*
1535. a. Burlington *Free Press*
1536. h. Newport *Daily Express*
1537. f. Rutland *Daily Herald*
1538. e. St. Albans *Messenger*
1539. b. St. Johnsbury *Caledonian-Record*
1540. d. *Addison County Independent*—WFAD
1541. c. *White River Valley Herald*—WCVR
1542. a. *Springfield Reporter*—WCFR
1543. b. *Vanguard Press*—WJOY
1544. a. C. Harry Behney—GBIC
1545. d. Louise Weiner—Vermont Retail Association
1546. b. Peter Foote—Associated Industries of Vermont
1547. c. Patricia Heffernan—Women Business Owners of Vermont
1548. Printer and bookbinder. He specializes in museum catalogues, scholarly journals, and limited edition volumes. Author and photographer Ethan Hubbard says he is "both the Rolls and the Royce of the business."
1549. d. Rutland
1550. a. Newport
1551. b. Brattleboro
1552. e. Montpelier
1553. c. Burlington
1554. f. St. Johnsbury
1555. e. Brandon
1556. f. Richford

1557. a. Middlebury
1558. c. Lyndonville
1559. b. Orleans
1560. d. Barton

1561.

According to the Vermont Historical Society, the first written description of "Champ" appeared in

    a. 1609.
    b. 1819.
    c. 1902.
    d. 1974.

Answer

    a. 1609

Samuel de Champlain describes a Champ-like creature in his journal. He said it was about twenty feet long and had a head like a horse. Leon W. Dean called "Champ" Lake Champlain's "ace in the hole" in 1959 and reports the following newspaper account from 1871. "The 'What is it?' of Lake Champlain was again interviewed near Barber's Point on Monday last. It was in full view of the passengers of the steamer Curlew."

On April 29, 1986, the senate adopted a resolution encouraging "serious scientific inquiry into the existence of any unusual animal in Lake Champlain, especially the possible existence of any such as the one commonly known as 'Champ.' "

CHAPTER 26

Rocky Vermont

Realtors in Vermont will tell you the key questions people ask before buying property here are: Is there a fireplace? and Is there a view of the mountains? In a sense our Green Mountains are a metaphor for the Vermont dilemma of the twenty-first century: Do people want Vermont to be a place to look at or to live with? We have argued elsewhere: "Rural means living with the earth. It means understanding a few things well. It means knowing a few people completely. It means patience with nature. It means, most of all *involvement* with the planet. One lives in the country to *be with* the mountains, not to look at them." How to be with our mountains in a human way and not sully them or detract from their majesty—a condition that is absolutely secure only when they are alone and apart from us. That is our challenge.

Rank the following mountains according to their height:

Highest

_____	1562.	a. Killington
_____	1563.	b. Mt. Ellen
_____	1564.	c. Mansfield
_____	1565.	d. Camel's Hump

Lowest

1566. Where is the "Valley of Vermont" located?

The answers to Chapter 26 begin on page 268.

a. Between Winooski and Montpelier
b. Between Lake Willoughby and Burke Mountain
c. Between Sharon and the New Hampshire border
d. Between Brandon and the Massachusetts border

1567. What is called the "Grand Canyon of New England"?

a. Huntington Gorge
b. Quechee Gorge
c. Devil's Gulch in Eden
d. East Putney Falls and Pot Holes

1568. You are hiking the Long Trail. Which peak won't you cross?

a. Ascutney
b. Pico
c. Jay
d. Camel's Hump

1569. The Green Mountains are younger than the Adirondacks.

a. True
b. False

1570. The name "Vermont" means

a. an ever-green mountain.
b. green mountains.
c. a mountain of maggots.
d. a or c.

1571. Camel's Hump has also been known as

a. Camel Mountain.
b. The Couching Lion.
c. Mount Camel.
d. The Sleeping Camel.

1572. Prominent parts of Mt. Mansfield are known as

a. the Father, the Child, the Mother.
b. the Forehead, the Nose, the Chin.
c. the House, the Woodpile, the Shed.
d. the Peak, the Summit, the Ridge.

1573. In 1934 the Civilian Conservation Corps was responsible for

a. putting a road through Smugglers' Notch.

b. putting out a severe forest fire in Stowe.

c. cutting several ski trails on Mt. Mansfield.

d. the completion of the "Long Trail."

1574. Which of the following is *not* a mountain in Vermont?

a. Blue Ridge Mountain

b. Salt Ash Mountain

c. Mount Jefferson

d. Mother Myrick Mountain

1575. The Union High School in Bristol is named after a mountain. Which one?

a. Union Mountain

b. Mt. Anthony

c. Mt. Abraham

d. Shaker Mountain

1576. How long is the Long Trail (not counting the side trails)?

a. 63 miles

b. 163 miles

c. 263 miles

d. 463 miles

1577. Which is higher, Burke Mountain or Mount Ascutney?

1578. Glastenbury Mountain is located in which part of the state?

a. North

b. South

c. East

d. West

1579. In Addison County, there is a mountain named for poet

_____.

1580. Hoosac Mountain is in which county?

a. Windham County

b. Bennington County

c. Washington County

d. Rutland County

1581. There are two major hiking trails that run along the spine of the Green Mountains. One is the Long Trail. What is the other?

1582. The Red Clover Trail is a famous branch of the Long Trail.

   a. True
   b. False

1583. What do Cochran, Carinthia, and Hogback all have in common?

1584. The scenic rock profiles at Smugglers' Notch are known as

   a. the Hunter and His Dog.
   b. the Smuggler and His Treasure.
   c. Man and Indian.
   d. the Old Man in the Mountain.

1585. The northeastern corner of Vermont is called

   a. the Northeastern Highlands.
   b. the Granite Hills.
   c. the Northeast Kingdom.
   d. all of the above.

1586. If you stay at Taft Lodge, you are hiking on

   a. Camel's Hump.
   b. Mt. Mansfield.
   c. Stratton Mountain.
   d. Jay Peak.

1587. If you hike up to Griffith Lake near Danby to go camping, be sure you bring

   a. money.
   b. a tent.
   c. a first-aid kit.
   d. all three.

1588. He lived on a farm on Camel's Hump in Duxbury. The
   _____ Skyline Trail is named after him. He constructed the last forty-eight miles of the Long Trail himself. His name is

   _____.

Match the mountain with the trail found on it:

_____ 1589. Bread Loaf Mountain   a. The Brownsville Trail
_____ 1590. Ascutney   b. Burr–Burton Trail
_____ 1591. Mt. Equinox   c. Clara Bow Trail
_____ 1592. Mt. Mansfield   d. Burnt Hill Trail

1593. Which mountain doesn't fit?

     a. Mt. Mansfield
     b. Camel's Hump
     c. Pico Peak
     d. Mt. Equinox

1594. The Green Mountain Club was founded in

     a. 1860.
     b. 1910.
     c. 1932.
     d. 1948.

Match the mountain with the mountain nearest it:

_____ 1595. Mt. Mansfield   a. Pico
_____ 1596. Killington   b. Belvidere Mountain
_____ 1597. Jay Peak   c. Dewey Mountain
_____ 1598. Burke Mountain   d. Kirby Mountain

Determine the name of the Vermont mountain based on a location and a hint:

1599. _____ Mountain (Avery's Gore)
     Hint: Square pegs won't fit in it.

1600. Mt. _____ (Holland)
     Hint: Mr. _____ Doe.

1601. _____ _____ Mountain (Dorset)
     Hint: What sits on a hooter's shoulders?

1602. _____Mountain (Barnet)
     Hint: Jimmy Stewart's rabbit (also a lake).

1603. _____ Mountain (Sandgate)
     Hint: Poached or Benedict.

1604. _____ Mountain (Starksboro)
     Hint: You put salt in one.

1605. _____ Mountain (Goshen)
    Hint: Lovers say there isn't enough of it anymore.

1606. _____ Mountain (Sharon)
    Hint: Actress Mary _____ Moore.

1607. _____ Hill (Pittsford)
    Hint: Fats (among others) found his thrill here.

1608. _____ Mountain (Benson)
    Hint: Think fence posts.

1609. _____ Mountain (Bridgewater)
    Hint: Yul or Eagle.

Match the town with the material found in the mountains there.

_____ 1610. Strafford   a. asbestos
_____ 1611. Danby   b. gold
_____ 1612. Barre   c. copper
_____ 1613. Hyde Park   d. granite
_____ 1614. Poultney   e. slate
_____ 1615. Plymouth   f. marble

1616. Hor and Pisgah are mountains looking at each other from the opposite sides of

    a. Lake Dunmore.
    b. Whitingham Reservoir.
    c. Lake Willoughby.
    d. Lake Raponda.

1617. In Salisbury there is a cave named for

    a. Thomas Chittenden.
    b. Ethan Allen.
    c. Seth Warner.
    d. Vincent Naramore.

1618. The Indian name for this mountain is "Long View in All Directions." The mountain is?

    a. Burke Mountain
    b. Mount Mansfield
    c. Jay Peak
    d. Glastonbury Mountain

266

1619. This mountain's name is formed from two Indian words meaning "the place where the top is." The name of the mountain is?

    a. Camel's Hump
    b. Mt. Equinox
    c. Hogback Mountain
    d. Mt. Ascutney

1620. He founded the Green Mountain Club and the Long Trail. His life, according to Vrest Orton in 1950, was "one of the most selfless and most useful lives of any public figure in Vermont." He once drew attention by suggesting (as a member of the Vermont Academy faculty in Saxtons River) that no boy should be allowed to graduate from a Vermont high school until he had climbed at least one Vermont mountain. Edward Crane, who edited the *Burlington Free Press*, said of him:

    "In him were combined the vision
    Of a prophet
    The determination of a full day
    And the driving force of a battering ram.
    He believed in the power of ideas!"

    His name was ————————————————.

1621. Many of Vermont's principal mountains share the same name. Of the following names, which is the most popular?

    a. Bald
    b. Bear
    c. Green
    d. Spruce
    e. White Rocks

Answers:
Rocky Vermont

1562. c. Mt. Mansfield—4,393 feet
1563. a. Killington—4,241 feet
1564. b. Mt. Ellen—4,135 feet
1565. d. Camel's Hump—4,083 feet
1566. d. It's 85 miles long from Brandon to Massachusetts
1567. b. Quechee Gorge
1568. a. Ascutney
1569. a. True
1570. d. One story is that the Rev. Samuel Peters named the state Verd
       Mont from atop Mount Pisgah. Charlie Morrissey, a well-
       known "Vermontist," writes "Peters . . insisted that he named
       the state Verd Mont, for Green Mountain, not Vermont, which
       translates from the French as 'Mountain of Maggots.' Piqued at
       his critics he curtly observed: 'If the former spelling is to give
       way to the latter, it will prove that the state had rather be con-
       sidered a mountain of worms than an ever green mountain.' "
1571. b. The Couching Lion. (It has also been called Camel's Rump.)
1572. b. the Forehead, the Nose, the Chin.
1573. c. Cutting ski trails.
1574. c. Mount Jefferson is in New Hampshire; all the others are
       mountains that are in Vermont.
1575. c. Mt. Abraham
1576. c. 263 miles
1577. Burke Mountain by 123 feet.
1578. b. South (flatlanders might also say west).
1579. Robert Frost
1580. b. Bennington County
1581. The Appalachian Trail
1582. b. False. The Department of Agriculture puts out a list of Ver-
       mont farms that welcome visitors. This list is known as the
       Red Clover Trail.
1583. They are three ski areas.
1584. a. the Hunter and His Dog.
1585. d. all of the above.
1586. b. Mt. Mansfield.
1587. d. all three. There is no camping within two hundred feet of the
       lake anywhere and tents may be pitched only at designated
       sites. All this is overseen by a caretaker. While such policies are
       necessary, it sure snatches away a bit of the romance.

1588. Monroe, Will S. Monroe

1589. d. Bread Loaf Mountain—Burnt Hill Trail

1590. a. Ascutney—The Brownsville Trail

1591. b. Mt. Equinox—Burr–Burton Trail

1592. c. Mt. Mansfield—Clara Bow Trail

1593. d. Mt. Equinox is not in the Green Mountains. It is in the Taconic Mountain range.

1594. b. 1910. All Vermonters should give thanks for the Green Mountain Club. It has quietly and without fanfare or strident politics protected our great treasure. It maintains 440 miles of footpaths in Vermont. Its purpose is "to make the mountains of Vermont play a larger role in the lives of people."

1595. c. Mt. Mansfield—Dewey Mountain

1596. a. Killington—Pico

1597. b. Jay Peak—Belvidere Mountain

1598. d. Burke Mountain—Kirby Mountain

1599. Round

1600. John

1601. Owl's Head

1602. Harvey

1603. Egg

1604. Shaker

1605. Romance

1606. Tyler

1607. Blueberry

1608. Cedar

1609. Bald

1610. c. Strafford—copper

1611. f. Danby—marble. (The Danby marble quarry is the largest underground quarry in the United States. As of 1978, twenty-two acres had been carved from inside Dorset Mountain. The United States Supreme Court Building, the Oregon State Capitol, the Dirksen Senate Office Building, and the Thomas Jefferson Memorial were all built with Danby marble.)

1612. d. near Barre—granite

1613. a. Hyde Park—asbestos

1614. e. Poultney—slate

1615. b. Plymouth—gold

1616. c. Lake Willoughby

1617. b. Ethan Allen

1618. a. Burke Mountain

1619. b. Mt. Equinox, from the Indian words Agwanok Ewanok.

1620. James P. Taylor

1621. a. There are six mountains in Vermont, all over two thousand feet, named Bald. (There are also six named Burnt.) There are seven that have the name "Little" such as Little Equinox and Little Wilcox Peak. There are five Spruce, four White Rocks, three Green, and two Bear.

1622.

Who was Lloyd E. Squire?

Answer

The "Old Squire" died in Waterbury, Vermont, on November 1, 1979. He founded (with Harry Whitehill) WDEV in Waterbury. Thousands and thousands of Vermonters listened as the Old Squire read from his own poems and those of Daniel Cady. He helped give Vermont a radio station that has never lost its local character, its human scale, or its sense of place. Along with Rusty Parker and others, Lloyd Squire accompanied an entire generation of farm boys through life from the first time they shoveled out from behind the cows (at the age of six or seven) to the time they "took over the milking." Their voices are engraved in our "memories of the heart."

A DOZEN OR SO
QUESTIONS ABOUT TOWN GOVERNMENT

1623. If you run for justice of the peace and accept contributions or make expenditures of $500 or more, you must file three campaign finance reports.

    a. True
    b. False

1624. If you are married by a justice of the peace in Vermont, you must pay her or him

    a. $10 per person—usually that means $20.
    b. $25 between 9 A.M. and 7 P.M.
       $50 between 7 P.M. and 9 A.M.
    c. $25 anytime.
    d. whatever you damn well please.

1625. On average, in towns of under 2,500 population, about _____ of a town's registered voters will be in attendance at town meeting.

    a. 10%
    b. 25%
    c. 45%
    d. 60%

1626. In a Vermont town, the list of items to be resolved at a town meeting is called the _____.

1627. You are at town meeting. There is an election for a town office. The result is Jones–60, Smith–50, and Brown–40. What happens next?

    a. Jones is declared the winner.
    b. Smith goes home mad.
    c. There is another election between Jones, Smith, and Brown.
    d. The second choices on Brown's ballots are distributed between Jones and Smith.
    e. a and b.

The answers to this section begin on page 274.

1628. In 1936 on town meeting day, Vermonters voted "No" (30,795 "for" and 42,873 "against") to a proposed public works project for the state. What was it?

1629. Town meeting day is set by Vermont law as

    a. the first Tuesday in March.
    b. the first Tuesday after the first Monday in March.
    c. either the first Monday or Tuesday in March—whichever the town chooses.
    d. the first day of sugaring season.

1630. The "quorum" at a Vermont town meeting is

    a. 5% of registered voters in attendance.
    b. 5% of eligible voters in attendance.
    c. 10% of registered voters in attendance.
    d. There is no specified percentage of citizens needed to conduct a town meeting.

1631. What is the first order of business at every town meeting?

1632. Road commissioners are

    a. always elected at town meeting.
    b. always appointed by the selectmen.
    c. elected unless a vote is taken to have the selectmen appoint.
    d. appointed by the selectmen unless the town votes to elect.

1633. If you want to have an issue placed on the formal list of items to be resolved, you may do so by having _____ of the voters sign a petition supporting you.

    a. 5%
    b. 10%
    c. 15%
    d. 20%

1634. In towns of under 2,500 population, about _____ of those present at a town meeting are apt to participate verbally (not counting the seconding of a motion) at least once.

    a. 20%
    b. 40%
    c. 55%
    d. 65%

1635. Charles Kuralt of CBS "On the Road" fame and "Sunday Morning" was once asked what his favorite place in all America was. He said he found it in _____, Vermont, on Town Meeting Day.

1636. Thomas Jefferson once said that town meeting was "the wisest invention ever devised by the wit of man for the perfect exercise of self-government."

a. True
b. False

Answers:
A Dozen or So
Questions about Town Government

1623. a. True
1624. d. whatever you damn well please.
1625. b. 25%
1626. warning
1627. c. But if no one gets a majority after three ballots, the moderator drops the lowest vote getter from the race.
1628. The Green Mountain Parkway Proposal
1629. a. the first Tuesday in March.
1630. d. There is no specified percentage.
1631. The election of the moderator (the person who conducts the town meeting).
1632. d. appointed by the selectmen unless the town votes to elect.
1633. a. 5%
1634. b. 40%
1635. Strafford
1636. a. True. Of course. Just wanted to get it in.

SCENES MOST APT TO
END UP ON A POSTCARD

Can you identify them?

1637. _____

1638. _____

The answers to this section begin on page 277.

1639. _____

Answers:
Postcard Scenes

1637. Placey Farm on Route 5 in Newbury, on the Connecticut River
1638. Village of East Corinth
1639. Strafford Meeting House

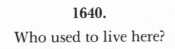

1640.

Who used to live here?

Answer

Ethan Allen.